The Medea of Seneca

Lucius Annaeus Seneca

THE

MEDEA OF SENECA

WITH AN

INTRODUCTION AND NOTES

BY

Hugh MacMaster Kingery, Ph.D.

PROFESSOR IN WABASH COLLEGE

REVISED EDITION

CRAWFORDSVILLE, IND.
PUBLISHED BY THE AUTHOR
1900

THE

MEDEA OF SENECA

WITH AN

INTRODUCTION AND NOTES

BY

Hugh MacMaster Kingery, Ph.D.

PROFESSOR IN WABASH COLLEGE

REVISED EDITION

CRAWFORDSVILLE, IND.
PUBLISHED BY THE AUTHOR
1900

Copyright 1900
HUGH MACMASTER KINGERY

PREFACE

The kindly reception accorded the first edition of this work encourages the author to believe that it meets an actual want. The demand, continued after the edition was exhausted, has led to the publication of this revision, which embodies the results of further study and of personal experience with the book in the classroom, as well as many helpful hints from others who have used it. The introduction and some of the notes have been condensed, other notes amplified, or new ones introduced, and all placed on the same page with the text.

The text is practically unchanged from the first edition, and the general plan of the notes remains the same.

WABASH COLLEGE, Nov. 1, 1900.

FROM THE PREFACE TO THE FIRST EDITION

The *Medea* has been chosen for presentation because of its comparative excellence and because its authenticity is almost unquestioned. In the preparation of the notes it has been assumed that the reader is familiar with the essentials of the language, and only such points of form and syntax are noticed as present unusual difficulty. No grammatical references are given. In dealing with the subject-matter the aim has been rather to suggest than to state, thus leaving much for the student's own research to develop. Above all has it been desired, by the insertion of necessary references to authorities and cross-references to the text, to guide him to a mastery of the play itself. For the mythology free use is made of Latin (and occasionally of Greek) sources of information. The reader should have at hand especially a good edition of Ovid's *Metamorphoses*.

The text is that of Leo (Berlin, 1879), the few variations therefrom receiving mention in the notes. The various readings of the manuscripts and the conjectures and emendations of editors have been omitted from this preliminary edition.

Most of the abbreviations used in the introduction and notes are self-explanatory, but the following may be less clear to the student:

Agam.: Agamemnon (Seneca).
Ann.: Annales (Tacitus).
Dial.: Dialogus de Oratoribus (Tacitus).
Epist.: Epistulae (Horace, Pliny).
Ger.: Germania (Tacitus).
H. C.: Horati Carmina.
H. Epd.: Horati Epodi.
H. S.: Horati Saturae.
Her : Heroides (Ovid).
Herc. Fur.: Hercules Furens (Seneca).
Herc. Oet.: Hercules Oetaeus (Seneca).
I. O.: Institutio Oratoria (Quintilian).

Med.: Medea (Euripides, Seneca).
N. D.: de Natura Deorum (Cicero).
N. H.: Naturalis Historia (Pliny).
Oct.: Octavia (Seneca).
Oed.: Oedipus (Seneca).
O, M.: Ovidi Metamorphoses.
O.R.A.: Ovidi Remedium Amoris.
Phaed.: Phaedra (Seneca).
S. or Sat.: Saturae (Horace, Juvenal).
Theb.: Thebais (Statius).
Thy.: Thyestes (Seneca).
Tro.: Troades (Seneca).
V. A.: Vergili Aeneis.
V. E.: Vergili Eclogae.

INTRODUCTION

ROMAN TRAGEDY FROM LIVIUS TO ACCIUS

For five centuries Rome had no literature, but about B. C. 240 Livius Andronicus, who had been a slave and now was a schoolmaster, being in want of a good Latin text book, translated the *Odyssey* of Homer into rude Saturnian verse. Finding this first essay successful he widened the scope of his adventure, and brought over some comedies and later some tragedies from the Greek. His success as tested by the popularity of his work was unquestioned, and, though little can be said for the originality or literary merit of his productions, it is from this beginning that the history of Roman literature dates.

The example thus set was not long in being followed. A host of translators and adapters sprang up, treading for the most part the comparatively narrow path marked out by the pioneer. Practice, under the spur of emulation, produced a gradual improvement in form and finish, and soon one and another ventured to introduce new features. Instead of translation, bald or free, came the interpolation of incidents and dialogue not in the original, the welding together of two plots (*contaminatio*) and the introduction of bits of local coloring which served to render the scenes more intelligible to the untraveled Roman. Especially was this true of the Comedy, as is seen in the plays, still extant, of Plautus and Terence.

In tragedy the earliest names after Livius are those of Nævius, Ennius and Pacuvius, all of whom were living within a quarter-century after the enterprising schoolman had made his debut. All borrowed freely from the Greek, as he had done. Presently, however, the Roman's national pride suggested an attempt at a national drama, and the result is seen in the *fabulae praetextae* of Nævius and his successors. In these, while the form of the Greek play was retained, both plot and characters were purely Roman. Such titles are met as the *Romulus* of Nævius, the *Paullus* of Pacuvius and the *Brutus* and *Aeneadae* of Accius.

Unfortunately we have of these earliest products of the Roman tragic muse nothing more than a list of titles and a few of the merest fragments—too little data for the formation of any independent judgment of their merits. For this we must rely on the authority of ancient critics who had access to the plays in their entirety. Cicero constantly professed a great admiration for Ennius, though rather as an epic than as a tragic poet. Varro is quoted as having declared Pacuvius a model of richness in diction. To Pacuvius and Accius Quintilian ascribes the first place among ancient tragic writers in vigor of thought and expression and in the dignity of the characters they created. The popularity enjoyed in the Augustan age by these old authors provoked the sarcastic protest of Horace (see especially *Epist.* 2, 1, 18-75). Roman critics generally admitted the courage and vigor of these pioneers in literature, while at the same time they deplored the rudeness of their style; but this, Quintilian observes, was due less to themselves than to their time.

DECLINE OF THE TRAGEDY AT ROME

The interest in tragedy was soon overshadowed by the growing popularity of the comedy, which appealed more powerfully to the Roman taste; and, while the comedies of Plautus and Terence were still popular in the time of Augustus, the custom of presenting tragedies on the stage very soon died out. A natural consequence was the diversion of literary effort into other channels, and in the half-century following the death of Accius there was but one tragic writer of any note —L. Julius Cæsar Strabo. After Accius, indeed, it is probable that works of this sort were composed rather as literary experiments, and for private reading or at most for declamation, than for exhibition on the stage. Many of the later poets tried their skill in this species of composition— among them Q. Cicero, Varro, Varius, Asinius Pollio, Ovid, Pomponius Secundus and Seneca— some with considerable success, if we accept the judgment of Quintilian (*I. O.* 10, 1, 98). In all we find mention made of thirty-six Roman poets who tried their hands at tragedy, and the number of their works mounts up to about one hundred and fifty.

THE SENECAN TRAGEDIES

Of all this mass of tragic literature we have to-day, aside from inconsiderable fragments, only the plays which bear the name of Seneca. Nine of the ten are adaptations from the Greek, while one

is a *praetexta*. Fortunately most of the Greek originals are extant, so that comparison with them is
possible—an advantage we do not enjoy in studying
the Latin comedy. Thus we find that the *Agamemnon* was borrowed from Aeschylus, the *Oedipus* from Sophocles, and no less than five of the
others—the *Medea*, the *Hippolytus* or *Phaedra*, the
Hercules Furens, the *Troades* or *Hecuba* and the
Phoenissae—from Euripides. It is worthy of note
that from the first it was not the solemn, stately
idealism of Aeschylus and Sophocles but the hu-
man realism of Euripides that most attracted the
Romans. From the time of Ennius down it was
Euripides who was copied oftenest.

In most cases the Senecan characters bear the
same names as in the Greek originals, and in
essential features are the same; though they differ
in points of detail and often are inferior in dis-
tinctness of conception and consistency of development. In plot the Roman author has not ventured
to vary far from his models, though here and
there he has altered the arrangement as well as
the allotment of space to the several scenes.
The *Hercules Furens* opens with a scene (not in
Euripides) in which Juno foreshadows the catastrophe, and the *Troades* is a contamination of
Euripides' *Hecuba* and his *Troades*. As a rule the
Latin plays are considerably shorter than their
Greek prototypes. New characters are not introduced, but frequently one or another is omitted.

The chorus is retained as in the Greek, although
(since the orchestral pit was occupied in the
Roman theater by seats for the senators) there
was no space provided for the choral dance. In

early times the chorus may have had a place on the stage, and its retention in tragic composition after public representation ceased was due probably to tradition and to the opportunity thus afforded for experiment in lyric passages. Horace's precept, *Actoris partes chorus..defendat*, can hardly be said to have been observed in these plays. There is little of that direct participation in the development of the plot which is assigned the chorus by the Greeks and especially by Aeschylus. Its part here is more formal and artificial—rather a set passage on some lyric theme suggested more or less remotely by the context than an integral part of the whole. In this as in the handling of characters our author carries to an extreme an innovation of Euripides.

The *Octavia* is constructed on the same general plan as the other nine tragedies, having its dialogue and its choruses, but differing, of course, in plot and scene, and presenting also some peculiarities of versification. Scholars are pretty generally agreed now that it is later than the age of Nero, though its author evidently was a close student of Seneca's thought and style.

While the Senecan tragedies are not arranged in trilogies, there are some pairs in which both plays contain the same principal characters. These are (1) the *Oedipus* and the *Phoenissae* or *Thebais*, in which the downfall and exile of the hapless Theban king are portrayed; (2) the *Thyestes* and the *Agamemnon*, whose theme is the house of Pelops and its dark destiny; and (3) the two plays in which the hero Hercules overshadows all other characters—the *Hercules Furens* and the *Hercules*

Oetaeus. The remaining plays are unconnected—
the *Hippolytus* or *Phaedra*, whose double title suggests its plot: the *Troades* or *Hecuba*, dealing with
the fortunes of the royal house after the fall of
Troy; and the *Medea*.

THE MEDEA

This play is regarded as one of the best of the
group. Title, plot and characters are taken from
Euripides. In both authors the scene is Corinth
and the time that of the heroine's repudiation and
revenge. In both are scenes in which she protests
to King Creon against the injustice of her banishment and gains from him the respite of a single
day; in which she seeks a final interview with
Jason, upbraids him with his faithlessness and
listens with scorn to his excuses; and in which,
having slain her two sons, she is borne away
through the air. In both she endeavors at first to
recall her recreant husband to his duty, and, fail-
ing in that, dissembles her wrath but begins at
once to plan her revenge.

Along with these points of resemblance are
many minor differences. Of the *dramatis personae*
Seneca omits entirely the *paedagogos* and Aegeus,
king of Athens, and makes the two boys, who in
the Greek play cry out behind the scenes when
attacked by their mother, purely mute characters.
The messenger who reports the catastrophe at the
palace also has a less important part, speaking but
ten lines in Seneca as against 103 in Euripides.
Medea's long address to the chorus, setting forth
her woes and her vengeful design, and the promise of silence on the part of the chorus (EUR. 216-

272), are omitted from the Latin play. So, of
course, is the interview with Aegeus (EUR. 661-
761). Other omissions of less extent occur, and in
their stead is inserted the scene (SEN. 670 848) in
which Medea's incantations are recorded at length.
The introduction of the *hymenaeus* as one of the
choruses is an innovation of the Latin author.
In matters of detail we find still further variations.
Thus in Euripides Medea is commanded (*v.* 275)
to take her children with her into exile, and with
pretended earnestness entreats her husband to ob-
tain a revocation of the edict (*vv.* 935·939); while
in Seneca it is she who desires them to go with
her, and her husband who insists that they re-
main. In the Greek she is determined to de-
stroy her husband as well as her rival (*vv.* 364-
376), but does not form the design until later
(*vv.* 787 ff.) of striking at him through their
sons; though in the very first scene the nurse
is represented as fearful of danger to the
children from the mother's frenzy. Neither of
these ideas appears in the Latin. In the older
play Jason is told of the intended gift to his bride,
while in the newer he knows nothing of it until
it has done its deadly work. In both versions the heroine is by far the strongest character, but she overshadows the rest more com-
pletely in the Latin. Jason in the one play (EUR.
593–597) affirms that his purpose in wedding the
Corinthian princess is to gain means of protection
and support for Medea and her children; in the
other (SEN. 434–436, 518–530) he frankly confesses
that fear is his motive. In the one case he is a
smooth-tongued egoist, in the other a self-confess-

ed coward.   In both (EUR. 476–487; SEN. 449–489)
she reminds him of all she has done and sacrificed
in his behalf, and paints his ingratitude in vivid
colors.   The passages are very similar in substance, though the Greek is a straightforward
narrative and the Latin more declamatory.   Jason's
reply is reported differently.   According to Euripides he proceeds to prove by argument (*vv*. 534–
541) that her service to him had not been so great
after all, and that in fact she had gained more
than she had lost in following him; while in the
Latin (*vv*. 490, 491) he tries to evade her claims by
setting up the pitiful counter-plea that by his
tears he had persuaded Creon to grant her exile
instead of death.   Her reply is scathing in its
irony: *Poenam putabam; munus ut video est fuga* (*v*.
492).   Euripides makes them meet a second time,
Seneca but once.

The existence of such differences has prompted
the suggestion that probably Seneca did not imi-
tate Euripides directly, but rather some later (perhaps Alexandrian) version of the play.   Of course
the myth of Medea was common property.   Before
Euripides there had been the *Medea* of Neophron,
and as many as five other Greek tragedies of the
same title are catalogued.   Among the Romans too it
was a favorite theme.   Ennius had used it; so probably had Mæcenas; and Ovid's *Medea* won high praise
from Quintilian and Tacitus (*Dial*. 12). It is probable, therefore, that our author had access to several
Latin versions of the *Medea*, as well as to more
than one in Greek.   Nor is it unlikely that his
conception and treatment of it were affected by
Ovid's.   There is a striking parallel between the

two authors in methods and results. Each wrote much and easily, and each appears to have cared mainly for effectiveness of form and to have been willing, if need were, to attain this at the sacrifice of substance. While we have not Ovid's tragedy, we have his epistle of Medea to Jason (*Her.* 12), from which we may infer something of his conception of the heroine. Now the resemblance between the Medea of this epistle and the Medea of Seneca's tragedy is too close to be mere coincidence, and moreover there are many expressions essentially and some literally the same. It is hard to avoid the conclusion that the Neronian author was influenced to considerable degree by the Augustan, and that some of the variations from Euripides may be accounted for in this way.

In modern times the tragedy of Medea has appeared in Italian and French, and even in German and English versions.

THE STAGE SETTING

Permanent theaters were long unknown at Rome. Of those that were finally built the general plan was the same. At one side of the building was the stage, very long and narrow, with a permanent background representing the street front of one or more houses which could stand for whatever scene the particular play required. Immediately before the stage and somewhat lower was a large space exactly semicircular, filled with seats for the magistrates and those of senatorial rank; and beyond these rose the *cavea*, or general seating, in semicircular tiers. The *cavea* would often accommodate many thousands of spectators.

There was no roof, though sometimes an awning was stretched overhead to keep off the heat of the sun.

For the *Medea*—supposing, what appears very unlikely, that it ever was put on the stage—the background would represent the palace of King Creon and the home of Medea side by side. Creon's entrance and exit would be through the door of his palace, Medea's through the door of her own house; and her final appearance would be on its flat roof. The incantations detailed in the fourth act would be performed on the stage before her house. The chorus may be thought of as present throughout the play.

Two elements were recognized in the text of the play—the *diverbium* or dialogue proper, and the *canticum* or part that was chanted to musical accompaniment. In the *Medea* the first chorus may be supposed to have been divided between two bands of singers, who chanted their parts responsively; and all the choruses, as well as the impassioned scenes in the fourth act, may be classed as *cantica*.

THE METRES OF THE MEDEA

Seneca forms the iambic senarius with great regularity. In the *Medea* the rules are followed with especial strictness. For the characteristic iambus ($\smile -$) the equivalent tribrach ($\smile \smile \smile$) may be substituted, except in the last foot. Here not infrequently a pyrrhic ($\smile \smile$) occurs, the final syllable being *anceps*. The substitution of a spondee ($--$) or either of its equivalents, the dactyl ($-\smile \smile$) or the anapest ($\smile \smile -$), is common in the odd-numbered feet (first, third and fifth), but does not occur in the sixth as it might do according to Horace's statement (*A. P.* 255-257). The scheme of the senarius, with the variations met in the *Medea,* is as follows (figures denoting the verse in which each foot is met first):

1	2	3	4	5	6
⏑ — 8	⏑ — 1	⏑ — 122	⏑ — 5	⏑ — 512	⏑ — 1
⏑ ⏑ ⏑ 53	⏑ ⏑ ⏑ 10	⏑ ⏑ ⏑ 13	⏑ ⏑ ⏑ 1		
— — 1		— — 1		— — 1	
⏑ ⏑ — 6	⏑ ⏑ — 488	⏑ ⏑ — 897		⏑ ⏑ — 11	
— ⏑ ⏑ 29		— ⏑ ⏑ 15		— ⏑ ⏑ 266	
					⏑ ⏑ 2

The fifth foot is almost invariably a spondee or an anapest. *Vv.* 488 and 670 can be treated as beginning with a proceleusmatic, and some scholars have declared that the anapest never occurs in the second place.

In the lyric passages are met a variety of metres. The first chorus (*vv.* 56-115), though but sixty lines in length, changes measure three times. First is a passage of nineteen lines in the minor asclepiad (as in *H. C.* 1, 1, etc.), then eighteen glyconics, then seventeen more asclepiads, and finally six dactylic hexameters. These measures do not differ in structure from the same as written by Horace.

It is in the second chorus (*vv.* 301-379) that we meet Seneca's favorite choral measure, the anapestic dimeter. The standard foot may give way to a spondee or (except in the fourth place) to a dactyl. The single lines are not regarded as independent, but as parts of a continuous whole. The

final syllable of each verse must always be long
(not so, however, in the *Octavia*); and, contrary to
the usual rule in Latin poetry, a final consonant
in one line makes position with an initial consonant in the next. Hiatus between successive verses,
which the Greeks never allowed in this measure,
is admitted by Seneca. In this play there are
five instances (following *vv.* 342, 348, 827, 828, 832).
One of these is a hemistich (half-verse), and in
two instances the hiatus is at the end of a sentence;
Seneca does not use the paroemiac, with which the
Greeks regularly concluded an anapestic passage.

The longest chorus proper is at the end of the
third act (*vv.* 579-669), and is a form of the sapphic
strophe. A break occurs at *v.* 660, where the measure can be restored by supplying one hemistich,
though the sense may require an additional stanza.
Taking the chorus as it stands in Leo's text (supplying, of course, the half-line in *v.* 660), we count
fourteen stanzas or strophes, seven of four lines
each, as in Horace, and seven of nine lines each,
the last of each strophe being an adonic. In *v.*
636 the arsis of the second foot is resolved, bring-
ing two dactyls in succession. The caesura, always masculine, occurs regularly in the third foot.

The brief chorus which closes the fourth act
(*vv.* 849–878) is composed of twenty-seven anacre-
ontics (iambic dimeter catalectic) and three verses
one syllable less (iambic dimeter brachycatalectic).
It is rigid in its construction, the only variation
from the iambus being the use of a spondee, and
in four cases an anapest, in the first foot. The
final syllable with two exceptions (*vv.* 852, 861—
each at the end of a sentence) is long, either by

nature or by position (often on account of an initial consonant in the following line).

The frenzied speech of Medea in *vv.* 740-848, while not nominally a chorus. presents all the characteristics of one, metrically and sentimentally. Verses 740–751 are in the trochaic tetrameter catalectic. Then follow nineteen lines (752–770) in the iambic trimeter, then sixteen iambics in which trimeter and dimeter alternate (771-787). and finally fifty-six lines in the anapestic dimeter, but with three monometers (811, 816, 832) interspersed. The last six verses of the speech are a reversion to the ordinary dramatic form.

Authorship of the Senecan Tragedies

While all the manuscripts ascribe these plays to 'Seneca,' several circumstances afford opportunity for the creation of a 'Senecan question' which critics have not been slow to embrace. The several theories advanced are (1) that the plays are the work of the well-known philosopher; (2) that some are his and the remainder from another hand—or hands; (3) that all are the result of collaboration by Marcus and Lucius Seneca, the latter's brother Mela and the poet Lucan; and (4) that all are the work of an entirely different person, whose real or assumed name was Seneca.

It is impossible here to discuss these theories at length. The opinion now prevails that the *Octavia* certainly is not Seneca's, and that the other tragedies, with the possible exception of the *Agamemnon* and the *Hercules Oetaeus*, are his. Of external evidence in support of this conclusion we have the mention of Seneca as a poet by Quintilian, Pliny

and Tacitus, the citation of the *Medea* as his by
Quintilian (see *v.* 453 n.), the ascription of four
other tragedies in this collection to him by well-
known writers in the early centuries of our era
(*Oedipus*, *Phaedra*, *Thyestes* and *Troades*), and the
negative fact that we have no proof of the existence of a separate Seneca *tragicus.* Of internal
evidence there is the occasional allusion to con-
temporary events in which Seneca was deeply
concerned; the close parallel in philosophical
principles and general tone of thought between
the tragedies and the prose works which are in-
disputably his; and the identity of literary style in
the tragedies and prose works.

The case of the *Octavia* is different. Its omis-
sion from the oldest manuscript, the fact that the
philosopher himself is one of the *dramatis personae*,
the remarkable forecasting of the fate (*vv.* 629–
631) which befell Nero three years after Seneca's
death, and certain peculiarities of style and metre,
all have been cited as going to prove a later ori-
gin; and while none of these arguments is conclu-
sive in itself, their cumulative force is considerable. Various dates have been assigned for its
composition, as early as Domitian's reign and as
late as Hadrian's or later, but no definite conclusion can be reached. Historically the *Octavia*
agrees almost perfectly with Tacitus. It is of
especial interest to us as the one example extant
of the *fabula praetexta.*

In regard to word-forms and syntax the
Latin of Seneca is essentially that of the Golden
Age. In his prose he uses constructions which
earlier were admissible only in poetry, and gives

this word and that a somewhat different shade of
meaning, but in the main the mastery of Cicero,
Vergil and Ovid gives one the key to Seneca's
grammar. It was in his rhetoric that he created
a new school. Ovid had made a beginning, but
Seneca went much further. Form became the essential thing. An affectation of brevity, a strain-
ing after antithesis and epigram, came to be the
characteristics of his work and that of his imita-
tors (see Quintilian's judgment, *I. O.* 10, 1, 129).
In spite, however, of undeniable faults of style,
there is much that is good and more that is pleas-
ing, and no study of the literature of Rome can afford to leave Seneca out of account.

The Works of Seneca

As was remarked by Quintilian (*I. O.* 10, 1, 129),
Seneca was a very prolific and versatile writer,
working in almost every department of literature.
Of the prose works there are twelve books of
'*dialogi*,' in which ethical themes are discussed,
mainly from the Stoic point of view; two books
de Clementia and seven *de Beneficiis*; an extensive
compilation entitled *Naturales Quaestiones*, discuss-
ing various natural phenomena; and 124 'epistles,'
really moral essays, addressed to Lucilius. There
is also a collection of short letters, indorsed as au-
thentic by St. Jerome, but now regarded as coun-
terfeit, which purport to have passed between
Seneca and the apostle Paul (eight written by
Seneca, six by Paul).

Altogether the prose writings of Seneca, count-
ing only those which are admitted to be genuine,
cover more than a thousand closely printed pages

in the Teubner text edition. From fragments, moreover, and citations in later writers, we know that he wrote extensively in the fields of science, philosophy and history, in addition to the works which have been preserved. Mention has been made also of letters addressed to Novatus, and it is well known that he composed many speeches and state papers for Nero. His literary activity, therefore, must have been very considerable.

The *Apocolocyntosis*, partly in prose, partly in verse, is the only example known to be extant of the *Satura Menippea*. Its theme is the search of the lately deceased emperor Claudius for his proper place in the other world, and while it displays a good deal of ingenuity and talent of a certain order, its flippancy and irreverence make it distasteful to the modern reader.

The purely poetical works ascribed to Seneca are the nine epigrams and the ten tragedies already discussed. All display skill in the use of metrical forms, without, however, a high endowment of poetic genius.

MEDEA

DRAMATIS PERSONAE

MEDEA	IASON
NVTRIX	NVNTIVS
CREO	CHORVS

SCAENA CORINTHI

ACT I

[A street in Corinth. In the background are the palace of King Creon and the home of Jason and Medea. From the latter enters Medea, furious at Jason for his desertion of her and his marriage to the Princess Creusa (Glauce), which is set for that day.]

MED. Di coniugales tuque genialis tori,
Lucina, custos quaeque domituram freta
Tiphyn novam frenare docuisti ratem,
et tu, profundi saeve dominator maris,
clarumque Titan dividens orbi diem,   5
tacitisque praebens conscium sacris iubar

---

2. **Lucina:** the bringer-to-light—an epithet often applied to Diana and also to Juno. **quaeque...docuisti:** Pallas (Minerva). It was under her direction that the materials were chosen and the Argo built (cf. *vv.* 365-367).   3. **Tiphyn:** the Argo's pilot. For his fate see *vv.* 616-624. **novam:** The Argo was thought of as the first Grecian vessel to attempt a long sea voyage.   4. **profundi. dominator maris:** Neptune (cf. *dominus profundi, v.* 597).   5. **Titan:** Helios, the sun-god. In *v.* 410 Enceladus is thus designated. **orbi:** sc. *terrarum. Orbi* is indirect object of *dividens* (cf. *feminis...carmina divides,* H. C. 1, 15, 14).   6. **Taci-**

Hecate triformis, quosque iuravit mihi
deos Iason, quosque Medeae magis
fas est precari: noctis aeternae chaos,
aversa superis regna manesque impios   10
dominumque regni tristis et dominam fide
meliore raptam, voce non fausta precor.
nunc, nunc adeste, sceleris ultrices deae,
crinem solutis squalidae serpentibus,
atram cruentis manibus amplexae facem;   15
adeste, thalamis horridae quondam meis
quales stetistis: coniugi letum novae
letumque socero et regiae stirpi date.
mihi peius aliquid, quod precer sponso, manet:
vivat. per urbes erret ignotas egens   20
exul pavens invisus incerti laris,
iam notus hospes limen alienum expetat,
me coniugem optet quoque non aliud queam
peius precari, liberos similes patri
similesque matri—parta iam, parta ultio est: 25

---

tis sacris: the silent mysteries of night. 7. **Hecate triformis**: cf.
fronte non una, v. 751; *triceps Hecate,* O. M. 7, 194; *diva triformis,* H. C. 3,
22, 4. This goddess was thought of as having functions in heaven, on earth
and in the infernal world. She was identified or confused, therefore, with
Selene or Phoebe (Luna), with Artemis (Diana), and with Persephone
(Proserpina). 10. **Manesque impios**: ghosts of the wicked dead,
who are invoked along with their rulers, Pluto and Proserpina. 11.
dominum: Pluto. **dominam...raptam**: Proserpina, who had been
carried off by Pluto and made his bride (O.M. 5, 359-424), but not deserted
later as Medea had been; hence the phrase 'with better faith' **voce non
fausta**: because invocation of the powers of darkness was *nefas.* 13.
adeste: 'Be present to aid'—a common form of invocation (cf. *ades, v.*
703). **deae**: the Furies (Alecto, Megaera and Tisiphone), whose duty it
was to torment men for their evil deeds. For their characteristics cf. *vv.*
959-961. 17. **coniugi...novae**: the princess Glauce or Creusa, whom
Jason was about to marry. 18. **socero**: king Creon. **regiae stirpi**:
the whole royal house of Corinth. 19. **mihi peius aliquid**: Having
called down destruction upon her rival's family, she now prays that a
fate still worse may befall her faithless husband (cf. with *vv.* 20-25
Dido's curse on Aeneas, V. A. 4, 612-620). 22. **hospes**: a stranger or
guest, i. e. homeless. 24. **similes...matri**: like their father (in faith-

peperi.   querelas verbaque in cassum sero?
non ibo in hostes?   manibus excutiam faces
caeloque lucem—spectat hoc nostri sator
sol generis, et spectatur, et curru insidens
per solita puri spatia decurrit poli?   30
non redit in ortus et remetitur diem?
da, da per auras curribus patriis vehi,
committe habenas, genitor, et flagrantibus
ignifera loris tribue moderari iuga:
gemino Corinthos litore opponens moras   35
cremata flammis maria committat duo.
hoc restat unum, pronubam thalamo feram
ut ipsa pinum postque sacrificas preces
caedam dicatis victimas altaribus.
per viscera ipsa quaere supplicio viam,   40
si vivis, anime, si quid antiqui tibi
remanet vigoris; pelle femineos metus
et inhospitalem Caucasum mente indue.

lessness), like their mother (in wickedness and desolation).   26. peperi: Had Medea already some idea of the means by which she finally
punished her faithless husband (cf. *vv.* 549, 550)? querelas...sero: It
is time for action, not for words.   27. manibus: dat.—from their
hands. faces: carried in the marriage procession.   28. caelo: same
construction as *manibus*. Medea was credited (O.M. 7, 207-209) with having power to darken the heavens. spectat...poli: 'Does he see this, and
does he still show his face and pass on in his wonted course?' The allusion is to the sun's having hidden his face and retraced his course in horror at sight of the feast of Thyestes. nostri sator generis: Phoebus,
who was the father of Aeetes and hence grandfather of Medea.   35.
Corinthos: nom. gemino...litore: abl. quality. Cf. *bimaris Corinthi*, H. C. 1, 7, 2. opponens moras: by compelling vessels to sail
around the Peloponnesus (cf. *flectens moras, v.* 149). Many attempts
were made in ancient times to pierce the isthmus, but it was not until our
own day (1894) that a canal was completed. It follows the line surveyed
in 67 A. D. for Nero, who himself broke ground for it (Suetonius, Nero
19).   36. cremata: nom., agreeing with *Corinthos*. flammis ..duo:
unite the two seas with flame.   37. pronubam...pinum: a torch (cf.
faces, v. 27) borne by a young matron in the marriage procession. *Pronubam* here is adjective.   40. per viscera ipsa: the entrails of the victims on the altar—a common method of divination.   43. Caucasum:

quodcumque vidit Pontus aut Phasis nefas,
videbit Isthmos. effera, ignota, horrida,　　45
tremenda caelo pariter ac terris mala
mens intus agitat: vulnera et caedem et vagum
funus per artus—levia memoravi nimis:
haec virgo feci; gravior exurgat dolor:
maiora iam me scelera post partus decent.　　50
accingere ira teque in exitium para
furore toto. paria narrentur tua
repudia thalamis: quo virum linques modo?
hoc quo secuta es. rumpe iam segnes moras:
quae scelere parta est, scelere linquenda est domus.　　55

CHORVS

Ad regum thalamos numine prospero
qui caelum superi quique regunt fretum
adsint cum populis rite faventibus.
primum sceptriferis colla Tonantibus
taurus celsa ferat tergore candido;　　60
Lucinam nivei femina corporis
intemptata iugo placet, et asperi
Martis sanguineas quae cohibet manus,

i. e., the coldness and hardness of the Caucasus.　45. **effera, ignota,** etc.: neuter.　44. Scan as follows: *funus | per ar | tus levi | a memo | ravi | nimis.* The third foot is a dactyl, the fourth a tribrach.　49. **haec feci**: 'All this I did as a girl' (cf. *v.* 909). **exurgat**: *exsurgat.*　51. **accingere**: middle voice—'Gird yourself.'　52. **paria...thalamis**: Her marriage with Jason had involved the betrayal of her father and the murder of her brother. She now proposes to celebrate her repudiation with crimes as dreadful.　54. **hoc**: sc. *modo.*　59. **Tonans**: the proper epithet of Jupiter, here extended to his sister-wife as well.　61. **femina**: sc. *bos.* **nivei...corporis**: gen. quality, which here does not differ in force from the ablative in *tergore candido* above. To *di superi* were offered white victims (black to *di inferi*), which had never been used as beasts of burden (hence *intemptata iugo, v.* 62).　62. **placet**: from *placare,* not *placere.*　63. **quae...retinet**: Either Pax, the goddess of peace, or Pallas, representing scientific warfare as contrasted with Ares,

quae dat belligeris foedera gentibus
et cornu retinet divite copiam, 65
donetur tenera mitior hostia.
et tu, qui facibus legitimis ades,
noctem discutiens auspice dextera
huc incede gradu marcidus ebrio,
praecingens roseo tempora vinculo. 70
et tu quae, gemini praevia temporis,
tarde. stella, redis semper amantibus:
te matres, avide te cupiunt nurus
quam primum radios spargere lucidos.

Vincit virgineus decor 75
longe Cecropias nurus
et quas Taygeti iugis
exercet iuvenum modo
muris quod caret oppidum,
et quas Aonius latex 80
Alpheosque sacer lavat.
si forma velit aspici,
cedent Aesonio duci
proles fulminis improbi
aptat qui iuga tigribus, 85
nec non, qui tripodas movet,

the god of brute force (cf. Il. 5, 840; 21, 406; H. C. 3, 4, 53 ff.). 67.
tu qui...ades: Hymen (cf. v. 110). facibus legitimis: dat. Hymen
was invoked in song at all Greek weddings (see v. 116 n.) 71. tu quae...
redis: Hesperus, the evening star. Cf. *Vesper...expectata diu vix tandem
lumina tollit* (Catullus 62, 2). gemini praevia temporis: forerunner
of the twilight (cf. *dux noctis, v.* 878). 76. Cecropias nurus: daughters of Cecrops, i. e., Athenian maidens. 79. muris quod caret oppidum: Sparta. 80. Aonius: Boeotian or Theban. 81. Al-
pheos: An Arcadian stream. The bride is said to outshine the maids
of all these regions. 82. forma: abl. 83. Aesonio duci: Jason.
84. proles fulminis improbi: Bacchus, referring to the manner in
which Jupiter visited Semele (O. M. 3, 253-315). 86. qui tripodas
movet: Phoebus Apollo, who inspired the Delphic and other oracles

frater virginis asperae.
cedet Castore cum suo
Pollux caestibus aptior.
sic, sic, caelicolae, precor,   90
vincat femina coniuges,
vir longe superet viros.

Haec cum femineo constitit in choro,
unius facies praenitet omnibus.
sic cum sole perit sidereus decor,   95
et densi latitant Pleiadum greges
cum Phoebe solidum lumine non suo
orbem circuitis cornibus alligat.

                    *   *

ostro sic niveus puniceo color
perfusus rubuit, sic nitidum iubar   100
pastor luce nova roscidus aspicit.
ereptus thalamis Phasidis horridi,
effrenae solitus pectora coniugis
invita trepidus prendere dextera,
felix Aeoliam corripe virginem   105
nunc primum soceris, sponse, volentibus.
concesso, iuvenes, ludite iurgio,

(cf. *vv.* 785, 786). 87. **virginis asperae**: Diana.   89. **Pollux caestibus aptior**: cf. Il. 8, 237; H. S. 2, 1, 26.   91, 92. **vincat superet**:
surpass, excel.   93. **haec**: the bride.   **constitit**: 'has taken her
place.'   95. **cum sole**: 'with (at) the coming of the sun.'   97.
Phoebe: the moon.   **non suo**: reflected.   98. The sense appears to
be incomplete here, and Leo suggests two lines to restore the probable
connection, as follows: *talem dum iuvenis conspicit, en rubor | perfudit
subito purpureus genas.*   101. **luce nova**: at dawn.   **roscidus**: moist
with dew after his night watch.   102. **Phasidis horridi**: gen. The
river's name represents here the country itself.   *Ereptus, solitus* and
trepidus, like *felix*, modify *tu*, the implied subject of *corripe* (*v.* 105).
105. **Aeoliam virginem**: Jason's bride, Creusa, was a descendant of
Aeolus, the son of Hellen—not Aeolus the ruler of the winds.   106.
Medea's father had opposed her passion for Jason. This time the intended father-in-law is willing.   107. **iurgio**: cf. *fescenninus, v.* 113.

hinc illinc, iuvenes, mittite carmina:
rara est in dominos iusta licentia.

Candida thyrsigeri proles generosa Lyaei,   110
multifidam iam tempus erat succendere pinum:
excute sollemnem digitis marcentibus ignem.
festa dicax fundat convicia fescenninus,
solvat turba iocos—tacitis eat illa tenebris,
si qua peregrino nubit fugitiva marito.   115

108. **hinc illinc...mittite carmina**: sing responsively, as in Catullus 62.   109. 'Rarely is such license allowed us against our betters.' 110. 'Fair and noble scion of Bacchus.' Hymen, the god of marriage, is said to have been the son of Bacchus and Venus (wine and love), though other accounts are given (see Cl. Dict., art. *Hymen*).   111. **multifidam ...pinum**: cf. *multifidas faces*, O. M. 7, 259.   113. **dicax...fescenninus**: cf. *procax fescenninus*, Catullus 61, 126. The 'fescennine verses,' containing rude banter (*iurgio, v.* 107) and coarse jokes, were used in very early times by the rustics of central Italy on various occasions of public merry-making, but restricted later to wedding feasts. To make a Corinthian chorus use the word of course involves an anachronism. Verse 113 is spondaic.   114. **illa**: Medea.   115. **si qua**: equivalent to the relative *quae*.

ACT II

MED. Occidimus, aures pepulit hymenaeus
          meas.
vix ipsa tantum, vix adhuc credo malum.
hoc facere Iason potuit, erepto patre
patria atque regno sedibus solam exteris
deserere durus? merita contempsit mea   120
qui scelere flammas viderat vinci et mare?
adeone credit omne consumptum nefas?
incerta vaecors mente vaesana feror
partes in omnes; unde me ulcisci queam?
utinam esset illi frater! est coniunx: in hanc 125
ferrum exigatur. hoc meis satis est malis?
si quod Pelasgae, si quod urbes barbarae
novere facinus quod tuae ignorent manus,
nunc est parandum. scelera te hortentur tua
et cuncta redeant: inclitum regni decus   130
raptum et nefandae virginis parvus comes
divisus ense, funus ingestum patri
sparsumque ponto corpus et Peliae senis

  116. **hymenaeus**: The chant of the marriage procession (cf. Catullus 61 and 62). 117. **vix adhuc credo**; a very natural touch. 119. **solam**: sc. *me*. 121. **scelere**: a word which Medea does not hesitate to apply to her own acts, e. g. in *vv.* 129, 135, 500, 1016 (cf. *nefas, v.* 122). **flammas**: *igneos tauri halitus, v.* 466. 122. 'Does he forsooth believe that my every resource of evil is exhausted?' 124. **queam**: subjunctive in impassioned question. 125. **est coniunx**: sc. *illi.* **in hanc ferrum exigatur**: 'Into her let the sword be plunged.' For the construction cf. Seneca, Consolatio ad Marciam 16, 3: *Tela quae (Fortuna) in Scipiones…exegit*; also *ferrum exigam, v.* 1006. 131. **parvus comes**: her brother, Absyrtus (cf. *v.* 473 n.). 133. **Peliae senis**: Jason's uncle, who had deprived him of his throne and sent him in search

decocta aeno membra: funestum impie
quam saepe fudi sanguinem, et nullum scelus 135
irata feci: movit infelix amor.

    Quid tamen Iason potuit, alieni arbitri
iurisque factus? debuit ferro obvium
offerre pectus—melius, a melius, dolor
furiose, loquere. si potest, vivat meus, 140
ut fuit, Iason; si minus, vivat tamen
memorque nostri muneri parcat meo.
culpa est Creontis tota, qui sceptro impotens
coniugia solvit quique genétricem abstrahit
natis et arto pignore astrictam fidem 145
dirimit: petatur, solus hic poenas luat
quas debet. alto cinere cumulabo domum;
videbit atrum verticem flammis agi
Malea longas navibus flectens moras.
NVTR. Sile, obsecro, questusque secreto
        abditos 150
manda dolori. gravia quisquis vulnera
patiente et aequo mutus animo pertulit,
referre potuit: ira quae tegitur nocet;

of the golden fleece. Medea on reaching Iolcos had shown her power in
restoring to youth her husband's aged father (O. M. 7, 162-293), and the
daughters of Pelias desired the same boon for their sire. Medea assented,
but when on her advice they had cut his body into bits and placed them in
a caldron (*aeno, v.* 666), she refused to do her part. It was in their flight
from the vengeance of Pelias' son Acastus that she and Jason came to
Corinth. **sparsum ponto:** see *v.* 473. 135. **nullum scelus irata
feci:** Not anger but love had prompted all her crimes. 136. **movit:**
sc. *scelera* or *me* 137. By a sudden turn of thought she is led to seek
excuses for her lover. **alieni...factus:** brought under another's direction and control (cf. *sui iuris*). **arbitri:** gen. of *arbitrium*. 142. **nostri...meo:** This confusion of number in the pronoun of the first person is
quite common, especially in colloquial Latin. .**muneri...meo:** my gift
his life. 144. **genetricem natis:** In Euripides (Med. 275) Medea
is ordered to take her children with her into banishment. Seneca (cf. *vv.*
284, 541-546) represents her as desiring to do so but forbidden by Jason. 146. **petatur:** sc. *Creo.* 149. **Malea:** a promontory at the
southeastern extremity of the Peloponnesus. **flectens moras:** cf.
opponens moras, v. 35. 153. **referre:** repay, take vengeance.

professa perdunt odia vindictae locum.

MED. Levis est dolor qui capere consilium
       potest . 155

et clepere sese: magna non latitant mala.

libet ire contra. NVTR. Siste furialem impetum,

alumna: vix te tacita defendit quies.

MED. Fortuna fortes metuit, ignavos premit.

NVTR. Tunc est probanda, si locum virtus
       habet. ' 160

MED. Numquam potest non esse virtuti locus.

NVTR. Spes nulla rebus monstrat adflictis viam.

MED. Qui nil potest sperare, desperet nihil.

NVTR. Abiere Colchi, coniugis nulla est fides

nihilque superest opibus e tantis tibi. 165

MED. Medea superest, hic mare et terras vides

ferrumque et ignes et deos et fulmina.

NVTR. Rex est timendus. MED. Rex meus
       fuerat pater.

NVTR. Non metuis arma? MED. Sint licet terra
       edita.

NVTR. Moriere. MED. Cupio. NVTR. Pro-
       fuge. MED. Paenituit fugae. 170

NVTR. Medea— MED. Fiam. NVTR. Mater es.
       MED. Cui sim vides.

NVTR. Profugere dubitas? MED. Fugiam, at
       ulciscar prius.

NVTR. Vindex sequetur. MED. Forsan inveni-
       am moras.

159 **Fortuna fortes metuit:** Cf. *fortes fortuna iuvat*, Pliny. Epist. 6, 16, where it is quoted, perhaps, from the *fortes fortuna adiuvat* of Terence (Phormio 203); also *audentes fortuna iuvat* (V. A. 10, 284); and *audentes deus ipse iuvat* (O. M. 10, 58⁸). 166. **hic:** here, in me. 169. **sint... edita:** 'No, though they spring from the earth'—alluding to the *terrigenae* (cf. *vv*. 469, 470), whom Jason had vanquished by her aid. 171. **fiam:** sc. *Medea* –'I shall become Medea.' (cf. *Medea nunc sum*, v. 910). **cui sim vides:** 'You see whose mother I am'—i. e. no one's, since my sons

NVTR. Compesce verba, parce iam. demens, minis
animosque minue: tempori aptari decet. 175
MED. Fortuna opes auferre, non animum potest.
sed cuius ictu regius cardo strepit?
ipse est Pelasgo tumidus imperio Creo.

[*Enter King Creon from his palace. At first he does
not see Medea, but soliloquizes.*]

CREO. Medea, Colchi noxium Aeetae genus,
nondum meis exportat e regnis pedem? 180
molitur aliquid: nota fraus, nota est manus.
cui parcet illa quemve securum sinet?
abolere propere pessimam ferro luem
equidem parabam: precibus evicit gener.
concessa vita est, liberet fines metu 185
abeatque tuta. [*Sees Medea.*] fert gradum contra
ferox
minaxque nostros propius affatus petit.
arcete, famuli, tactu et accessu procul,
iubete sileat. regium imperium pati
aliquando discat. vade veloci fuga 190
monstrumque saevum horribile iamdudum avehe?
MED. Quod crimen aut quae culpa multatur fuga?
CR. Quae causa pellat, innocens mulier rogat.
MED. Si iudicas, cognosce. si regnas, iube.
CR. Aequum atque iniquum regis imperium
feras. 195

have been taken away. 177. **cardo strepit**: The door of a Grecian
house was suspended not on hinges but on pivots (*cardines*), usually of
wood, whose turning in their sockets was far from noiseless. In the comedy the entrance of a character is often heralded by some allusion to the
creaking of the pivot. 179. **Aeetae genus**: for *Aeeta nata*, as often. 183, 184. **luem**: Medea. **gener**: Jason. 189. **iubete sileat**:
a post-Augustan usage for the more common *iubete eam silere*. 193.
Either *innocens* is ironical here, or it is said as a general truth—(only) an
innocent woman asks, etc. 194. **si iudicas**: 'If you are acting as
judge, hear the case; if as despot, utter your commands.' The reading is

MED.   Iniqua numquam regna perpetuo manent.

CR.   I, querere Colchis.   MED.   Redeo: qui
             avexit, ferat.

CR.   Vox constituto sera decreto venit.

MED.   Qui statuit aliquid parte inaudita altera,
aequum licet statuerit, haud aequus fuit.   200

CR.   Auditus a te Pelia supplicium tulit?
sed fare, causae detur egregiae locus.

MED.   Difficile quam sit animum ab ira flectere
iam concitatum quamque regale hoc putet
sceptris superbas quisquis admovit manus,   205
qua coepit ire, regia didici mea.

quamvis enim sim clade miseranda obruta,
expulsa supplex sola deserta, undique
afflicta, quondam nobili fulsi patre
avoque clarum Sole deduxi genus.   210

quodcumque placidis flexibus Phasis rigat
Pontusque quidquid Scythicus a tergo videt,
palustribus qua maria dulcescunt aquis,
armata peltis quidquid exterret cohors
inclusa ripis vidua Thermodontiis,   215

hoc omne noster genitor imperio regit.
generosa, felix, decore regali potens
fulsi: petebant tunc meos thalamos proci,
qui nunc petuntur.   rapida fortuna ac levis

disputed.   197. **Colchis**: dat. **qui avexit**: Jason.   199. **parte...
altera**: without hearing the other side.   200. **licet**: concessive, as
in *v.* 169.   201. **Pelia**: the Latin form of *Pelias*. For the sense of the
line cf. *v.* 133 n. A case of *argumentum ad hominem*.   202. **causae**:
used in its Roman legal sense of a case on trial (cf. *vv.* 242, 262).
egregiae: ironical.   208. **expulsa...deserta**: Notice the asyndeton,
which is very common in all the tragedies.   210. **avo**: cf. *v.* 28 n.; also
v. 512.   212. **Pontus**: *Pontus Euxinus*, the Black Sea. **a tergo
videt**: as one sailed toward the mouth.   213. **maria dulcescunt**:
Pliny (N. H. 4, 24) declares that the Danube (Hister, *vv.* 585, 763), on account of its swift current, sweetens the waters of the Euxine for forty
miles out. Cf. also Polybius 4, 41, 42.   218. **fulsi**: from *ful-
gere*.   219. **rapida**: contains the same root as *eripuit* (*v.* 220), and

praecepsque regno eripuit, exilio dedit.   220
confide regnis, cum levis magnas opes
huc ferat et illuc casus—hoc reges habent
magnificum et ingens, nulla quod rapiat dies:
prodesse miseris, supplices fido lare
protegere. solum hoc Colchico regno extuli, 225
decus illud ingens Graeciae et florem inclitum,
praesidia Achivae gentis et prolem deum
servasse memet. munus est Orpheus meum
qui saxa cantu mulcet et silvas trahit,
geminique munus Castor et Pollux meum est 230
satique Borea quique trans pontum quoque
summota Lynceus lumine immisso videt,
omnesque Minyae: nam ducem taceo ducum,
pro quo nihil debetur: hunc nulli imputo;
vobis revexi ceteros, unum mihi.   235
incesse nunc et cuncta flagitia ingere.
fatebor: obici crimen hoc solum potest,
Argo reversa. virgini placeat pudor
paterque placeat: tota cum ducibus ruet
Pelasga tellus, hic tuus primum gener 240
tauri ferocis ore flammanti occidet.
fortuna causam quae volet nostram premat,
non paenitet servasse tot regum decus.
quodcumque culpa praemium ex omni tuli,

suggests the same idea here (cf. *rapax fortuna*, H. C. 1, 34, 14). 220.
eripuit: sc. *me*. 222. **hoc**: *prodesse, protegere*. 225. **solum hoc**:
servasse; cf. *obici...reversa*, v. 237. 226, 227. **decus, florem, praesidia, prolem**: the Argonauts. 228. **memet**: subject of *servasse*.
Orpheus: For his fate see *v*. 625 ff. and note on *v*. 625. 231. **sati
Borea**: Calais and Zetes (cf. *Aquilone natos, v*. 634.) 233. **ducem...
ducum**: Jason. 235. **vobis**: for you, i. e., all the Greeks. **unum
mihi**: him alone for myself. 237. **crimen hoc solum**: that the
Argo has returned. *Argo* is nom. in opposition to *hoc*. 238. The tenses
in *vv*. 238-241 suggest the figure of vision—she is dwelling upon the scene
as if it were before her eyes. **placeat**: suppose it had pleased—condi-
tion. 240. **gener**: Jason. 244. 'All the reward of all my crimes

hoc est penes te.   si placet, damna ream;   245
sed redde crimen.   sum nocens, fateor, Creo:
talem sciebas esse, cum genua attigi
fidemque supplex praesidis dextrae peti:
iterum miseriis angulum ac sedem rogo
latebrasque viles: urbe si pelli placet,   250
detur remotus aliquis in regnis locus.
CR.   Non esse me qui sceptra violentus geram ·
nec qui superbo miserias calcem pede,
testatus equidem videor haud clare parum
generum exulem legendo et afflictum et gravi   255
terrore pavidum, quippe quem poenae expetit
letoque Acastus regna Thessalica optinens.
senio trementem debili atque aevo gravem
patrem peremptum queritur et caesi senis
discissa membra, cum dolo captae tuo   260
piae sorores impium auderent nefas.
potest Iason, si tuam causam amoves,
suam tueri: nullus innocuum cruor
contaminavit, afuit ferro manus
proculque vestro purus a coetu stetit.   265
tu, tu malorum machinatrix facinorum,
feminea cui nequitia ad audenda omnia,
robur virile est, nulla famae memoria,
egredere, purga regna, letales simul
tecum aufer herbas, libera cives metu,   270

---

is now in your possession.'   245. **damna**: imperative.   246. **redde
crimen**: Condemn the accused, if you will, but restore the object (Jason)
for which the crime was committed.   248. **peti**: *petii, petivi* (cf. *redit,
v.* 984)   256. **quippe**: This word, in connection with a relative as
here, or alone as in *v.* 438, introduces a clause of cause or reason.   257.
Acastus: son and successor of Pelias as king of Iolcos (*v.* 133 n). The
fear in which Jason stood of him is expressed in *vv.* 521, 526.   261·
piae: filial (see note on *pietas, v.* 438). Note antithesis of *piae* and
impium, and cf. Ovid (M. 7, 339) on the same theme: *His, ut quaeque pia
est, hortatibus impia prima est.*   265. **vestro**: identifying Medea with
the powers of evil which she invoked.   270. **herbas**: used in her

alia sedens tellure sollicita deos.

MED.   Profugere cogis?   redde fugienti ratem
et redde comitem—fugere cur solam iubes?
non sola veni.   bella si metuis pati,
utrumque regno pelle.   cur sontes duos   275
distinguis?   illi Pelia, non nobis iacet:
fugam, rapinas adice, desertum patrem
lacerumque fratrem, quidquid etiam nunc novas
docet maritus coniuges, non est meum:
totiens nocens sum facta, sed numquam mihi.   280

CR.   Iam exisse decuit.   quid seris fando moras?

MED.   Supplex recedens illud extremum precor,
ne culpa natos matris insontes trahat.

CR.   Vade: hos paterno ut genitor excipiam sinu.

MED.   Per ego auspicatos regii thalami toros, 285
per spes futuras perque regnorum status,
Fortuna varia dubia quos agitat vice,
precor, brevem largire fugienti moram,
dum extrema natis mater infigo oscula,
fortasse moriens.   CR.   Fraudibus tempus petis.

MED.   Quae fraus timeri tempore exiguo potest?

CR.   Nullum ad nocendum tempus angustum est
              malis.

MED.   Parumne miserae temporis lacrimis negas?

CR.   Etsi repugnat precibus infixus timor,
unus parando dabitur exilio dies.   295

---

magic rites (cf. *v.* 706 ff.).   271. **sollicita**: imperative. For thought
cf. *invadam deos, v.* 424; *vidi aggressam deos, v.* 673.   274. **non sola
veni**: cf. *qui avexit ferat, v.* 197, and *redde comitem, v.* 273.   276.
'For him, not for me, was Pelias slain.' Medea argues that Jason, who
had profited by her crimes, was at least equally guilty with herself, who
had done them. She puts it with still greater force to Jason himself (*vv.*
500, 501—cf. *sontes duos, v.* 275). 282. **illud**: explained by the clause
ne...trahat. 287. **dubia**: known to be nominative, because its final
syllable, in arsis of the fourth foot, must be short. 288. **moram**:
respite. 293. Do you deny me a respite (even one which is) too brief

MED.   Nimis est, recidas aliquid ex isto licet:
et ipsa propero.   CR.   Capite supplicium lues,
clarum priusquam Phoebus attollat diem
nisi cedis Isthmo.   sacra me thalami vocant,
vocat precari festus Hymenaeo dies.   [*Exit.*]   300

CHORVS

   Audax nimium qui freta primus
rate tam fragili perfida rupit
terrasque suas post terga videns
animam levibus credidit auris,   304
inter vitae mortisque vias   307
nimium gracili limite ducto.

   Candida nostri saecula patres   329
videre, procul fraude remota.   330
sua quisque piger litora tangens
patrioque senex factus in arvo,
parvo dives, nisi quas tulerat
natale solum, non norat opes: 334
nondum quisquam sidera norat,   309
stellisque quibus pingitur aether   310
non erat usus, nondum pluvias
Hyadas poterat vitare ratis,
non Oleniae lumina caprae

---

for my tears (at parting with my children)?   296.   'Tis more than
enough, though you should strike off a portion. **recidas**: *i* long. 299.
Isthmo: the abl. of place whence, used without a preposition, as in
names of towns (cf. *tectis, v.* 380; *penatibus, v.* 450). **sacra thalami**:
the marriage rites.   301-308. Cf. H. C. 1, 3, 9-12.   329. For the
Golden Age, of which some features are given in the following verses, cf.
Oct. 396-406; V. E. 4: O. M. 1, 89-112; H. Epd. 16, 41-64; Tibullus 1, 3,
33-46. **candida**: white, unspotted, pure.   331. **piger**: unambitious,
content (cf. Herc. Fur. 198)   333. **parvo dives**: a favorite idea with
Horace (cf. C. 2, 16, 13 ff.; 2, 18, 11 ff.: 3, 16, 39 ff., etc.).   309. **sidera**:
the constellations, by means of whose positions the sailor in ancient
times determined the points of the compass.   311. **pluvias Hyades**:
see Cl. Dict.   313. **Oleniae...caprae**: Amalthea, the nurse of the in-
fant Jove, described now as a beautiful woman (see Cl. Dict., artt. *Aega*

nec quae sequitur flectitque senex
Attica tardus plaustra Bootes,   315
nondum Boreas, nondum Zephyrus
nomen habebant.

Ausus Tiphys pandere vasto
carbasa ponto legesque novas
scribere ventis: nunc lina sinu   320
tendere toto, nunc prolato
pede transversos captare notos
nunc antemnas medio tutas
ponere malo, nunc in summo
religare loco, cum iam totos   325
avidus nimium navita flatus
optat et alto rubicunda tremunt
sipara velo.   328
bene dissaepti foedera mundi   335
traxit in unum Thessala pinus
iussitque pati verbera pontum
partemque metus fieri nostri
mare sepositum.

Amalthea), now as a she-goat, in either case translated to the skies and made a constellation. The season when it first became visible was stormy, hence the allusion in this passage. **315. plaustra:** the constellation *Ursa Major*, still known as 'Charles's wain' in England. Being near the pole it was an object of great interest to the mariner and is referred to constantly in the poets (cf. *vv.* 405, 696). **Attica:** One version of the myth regarding Bootes makes him Arcas the son of Callisto (cf. O. M. 2, 401-530, translated to heaven, while the other identifies him with Icarius, an Athenian, father of Erigone. This latter form would justify the adjective *Attica*, transferring the epithet from Bootes to the wagon he drives. **tardus:** because the constellation. close to the pole, appears almost motionless. **316. nondum...habebant:** cf. O. M. 1, 132. **318. Tiphys:** For his fate see *v.* 617 ff. **321. prolato...notos:** catch the breeze with yards trimmed, tack, sail close to the win l. **335. bene:** modifies *dissaepti*, not *traxit*—brought together the lands well (wisely) separated before (cf. H. C. 1, 3, 21 ff.). **336. Thessala:** because built and commanded by Jason, of the Thessalian town Iolcos. **338. partem metus:** There were terrors enough for man before. but his conquest of the sea added new ones. **339. mare sepositum:**

dedit illa graves improba poenas   340
per tam longos ducta timores,
cum duo montes, claustra profundi,
hinc atque illinc subito impulsu
velut aetherio gemerent sonitu,
spargeret arces nubesque ipsas
mare deprensum.   345
palluit audax Tiphys et omnes
labente manu misit habenas.
Orpheus tacuit torpente lyra
ipsaque vocem perdidit Argo.
quid cum Siculi virgo Pelori,   350
rabidos utero succincta canes,
omnes pariter solvit hiatus?
quis non totos horruit artus
totiens uno latrante malo?
quid cum Ausonium dirae pestes   ,   355
voce canora mare mulcerent,
cum Pieria resonans cithara
Thracius Orpheus solitam cantu
retinere rates paene coegit
Sirena sequi?   quod fuit hujus   360
pretium cursus?   aurea pellis
ma⁚ ͺsque mari Medea malum,

(formerly) an element apart.   340. **illa:** the Argo—*Thessala pinus, v.*
335.   342. **duo montes:** the Symplegades (*v.* 456; cf. *scopulos ra-*
gantes, v. 610).   34*l.* Let slip the tiller from his nerveless hand.   349.
vocem perdidit: referring to the figure-head of the Argo, hewn from
the speaking oak of Dodona and itself possessed of the power of speech.
350. **virgo:** Scylla (Homer, Od. 12, 73-100, 234-259; O. M. 14, 1-74;
V. A. 3, 420-428).   354. **totiens latrante:** barking from each of its
(six) throats. **malo:** monster.   355. **dirae pestes:** the sirens
(Homer, Od. 12, 52 ff).   357. **resonans:** sounding *back*, in contest
with the sirens.   360. **sirena:** acc. 'Orpheus almost compelled the
siren to follow, (though) wont to hold captive with her song the passing
ships.' For Orpheus' power see *vv.* 626-629; O. M. 10, 86 ff.; and Cl.
Dict. The alliteration in *vv.* 359-362 may be accidental, yet it is by

merces prima digna carina.

    Nunc iam cessit pontus et omnes
patitur leges: non Palladia   365
compacta manu regumque ferens
inclita remos quaeritur Argo—
quaelibet altum cumba pererrat;
terminus omnis motus et urbes
muros terra posuere nova.   370
nil qua fuerat sede reliquit
pervius orbis:
Indus gelidum potat Araxen,
Albin Persae Rhenumque bibunt—
venient annis saecula seris,   375
quibus Oceanus vincula rerum
laxet et ingens pateat tellus
Tethysque novos detegat orbes
nec sit terris ultima Thule.

no means uncommon in these tragedies.   363. **merces**: appositive to
pellis and *Medea*—'wares worthy the first ship.' The sin of overstepping
the bounds appointed by the Creator (cf. *v.* 335 n) has brought its own
punishment. *Merces* suggests that the myth of the Argo and the golden
fleece may represent allegorically the beginning of commerce for the
Greeks.   364. **nunc iam**: *now*, transferring the thought from the
Argo's time to that of the chorus, and perhaps in the poet's mind to his
own day, when commerce had attained such great proportions.   365.
Palladia: see *v.* 2 n.   Here abl.   369. **motus**: sc. ...   372 **orbis**:
cf. *orbi, v.* 5 n.   375-379. This passage would be more remarkable if we
could suppose that Seneca meant by it anything more than a vague refer-
ence to some ideal Atlantis, such as Plato had described. One fanciful
critic has suggested that the Spaniard Seneca is here foretelling the dis-
covery of America by his countryman Columbus!

Act III

[Enter Medea from her house, followed by the old nurse, who tries to calm her.]

Nutr.　Alumna, celerem　quo　rapis　tectis
　　　　pedem?　　　　　　　　　　　　　　　　380
resiste et iras comprime ac retine impetum.
　　Incerta qualis entheos gressus tulit
cum iam recepto maenas insanit deo
Pindi nivalis vertice aut Nysae iugis,
talis recursat huc et huc motu effero,　　　385
furoris ore signa lymphati gerens.
flammata facies spiritum ex alto citat,
proclamat, oculos uberi fletu rigat,
renidet: omnis specimen affectus capit.
quo pondus animi vergat, ubi ponat minas　391
haeret: minatur aestuat queritur gemit.　　390
ubi se iste fluctus franget? exundat furor.　392
non facile secum versat aut medium scelus;
se vincet: irae novimus veteris notas.
magnum aliquid instat, efferum immane impium:
vultum furoris cerno.　di fallant metum!

---

380. **tectis**: cf. *Isthmo. v.* 299 n.　381. **resiste**: intransitive—
'Pause.'　383. **maenas**: The *maenades* (*bacchantes, thyiades*) were
the female priests of Bacchus. famed for their wild orgies. In *v.* 806
Medea applies the term to herself (cf. *v.* 849).　**Nysae**: a city in India,
where, according to one account, Bacchus was reared. One of his Greek
names (Dionysus) has been supposed to be a derivative of this word.
391. The figure is that of a balance whose opposing weights are so nearly
equal it is doubtful which will go down.　393. **facile**: adjective.
394. **vincet**: outdo. **veteris**: as displayed in the cases of her brother

MED. [*to herself.*] Si quaeris odio, misera, quem
    statuas modum:
imitare amorem.   regias egone ut faces
inulta patiar?   segnis hic ibit dies,
tanto petitus ambitu, tanto datus?   400
dum terra caelum media libratum feret
nitidusque certas mundus evolvet vices
numerusque harenis derit et solem dies,
noctem sequentur astra, dum siccas polus
versabit Arctos, flumina in pontum cadent,   405
numquam meus cessabit in poenas furor
crescetque semper—quae ferarum immanitas,
quae Scylla, quae Charybdis Ausonium mare
Siculumque sorbens quaeve anhelantem premens
Titana tantis Aetna fervebit minis?   410
non rapidus amnis, non procellosum mare
Pontusve Coro saevus aut vis ignium
adiuta flatu possit imitari impetum
irasque nostras; sternam et evertam omnia.
    Timuit Creontem ac bella Thessalici ducis? 415
amor timere neminem verus potest.
sed cesserit coactus et dederit manus:

Absyrtus and her uncle Pelias.   397. **odio**: dat. **misera**: addressing herself. **quem**: interrogative.   898. **imitare amorem**: Copy
your love, which knew no bounds, but sacrificed all to itself. **faces**:
torches carried in the marriage procession, hence marriage—here that of
the princess Creusa to Jason.   401. Cf. O. M. 1, 12, 13: [*nec*] *cir-
cumfuso pendebat in aere tellus* | *ponderibus librata suis*.   403. **derit**:
deerit (cf. *derat, v.* 992).   404. **siccas**; never setting (lit., dry).
The *arctoe* (*ursa major* and *ursa minor*) at the latitude of Greece and
and Rome, as at our own, were always above the horizon—did not dip
into the surrounding ocean as constellations farther from the pole were
thought to do (cf. *vetitum mare, v.* 758).   410. **Titana**: acc. Enceladus,
who was buried alive beneath Mt. Aetna (V. A. 3, 578-582). Ovid (M. 5,
352) follows Aeschylus in making it Typhoeus who was thus punished.
The myths of the Titans and the Giants are greatly confused.   413.
impetum irasque: hendiadys.   415. **Thessalici ducis**: Acastus
(cf. *v.* 257), who had demanded that Medea be given up for punishment
for the murder of his father.   417. **cesserit...dederit**: suppose he

adire certe et coniugem extremo alloqui
sermone potuit—hoc quoque extimuit ferox:
laxare certe tempus immitis fugae 420
genero licebat—liberis unus dies
datus est duobus.   non queror tempus breve:
multum patebit.   faciet hic faciet dies
quod nullus umquam taceat—invadam deos
et cuncta quatiam. NVTR. Recipe turbatum
    malis, 425
era, pectus, animum mitiga. MED. Sola est quies,
mecum ruina cuncta si video obruta:
mecum omnia abeant.   trahere, cum pereas, libet.
NVTR.   Quam multa sint timenda, si perstas, vide:
nemo potentes aggredi tutus potest. 430

[*Enter Jason soliloquizing and not seen at first by
Medea.*]

JAS.   O dura fata semper et sortem asperam,
cum saevit et cum parcit ex aequo malam!
remedia quotiens invenit nobis deus
periculis peiora: si vellem fidem
praestare meritis coniugis, leto fuit 435
caput offerendum; si mori nollem, fide
misero carendum.   non timor vicit fidem,
sed trepida pietas: quippe sequeretur necem

has—cf. *placeat* v. 288.   418. **coniugem**: Medea.   419. **ferox**:
ironical, and rendered intensely emphatic by its unusual position and its
antithesis to *extimuit*.   422. **non queror**: Note the sudden change of
tone. 'I do not complain that the time is (too) short. It will go far.'
424. **nullus**: sc. *dies*.   428. **pereas**: The 'general' second person.
432. **malam**: agrees with *sortem*—'Evil alike when it smites and when
it spares.'   434. **fidem praestare**: show fidelity, i. e., be faithful.
437. **misero**: sc. *mihi*—apparent agent.   438. **pietas**: reverent
affection, commonly that of a child for his parents, here of a father for
his children.   In *v.* 779 *piae* is said of Althaea's affection for her brother;
in Oct. 52 and 737 it stands for the nurse's love for her foster child and in
Oct. 844 for the prefect's devotion to his imperial master. See also *vv.*

proles parentum.　sancta si caelum incolis,
Iustitia, numen invoco ac testor tuum:　　　　440
nati patrem vicere.　quin ipsam quoque,
etsi ferox est corde nec patiens iugi,
consulere natis malle quam thalamis reor.
constituit animus precibus iratam aggredi. [*Medea*
　　sees him.]
atque ecce, viso memet exiluit, furit,　　　　445
fert odia prae se: totus in vultu est dolor.
MED.　　Fugimus, Iason: fugimus—hoc non est
　　novum,
mutare sedes; causa fugiendi nova est:
pro te solebam fugere.　discedo exeo,
penatibus profugere quam cogis tuis:　　　　450
at quo remittis?　Phasin et Colchos petam
patriumque regnum quaeque fraternus cruor
perfudit arva?　quas peti terras iubes?
quae maria monstras?　Pontici fauces freti
per quas revexi nobilem regum manum　　　　455
adulterum secuta per Symplegadas?
parvamne Iolcon, Thessala an Tempe petam?
quascumque aperui tibi vias, clausi mihi—
quo me remittis?　exuli exilium imperas

545, 943. **quippe**: causal as in *v.* 256, but here unaccompanied by
another connective. **sequeretur**: lit. follow, hence share.　441.
ipsam: Medea—so *iratam, v.* 444.　444. **animus**: sc. *meus.*　445.
viso memet: abl. abs.—at sight of me.　446. **fert...prae se**:
displays, exhibits. **odia**: plural of an abstract noun, where we should
use the singular.　447. **hoc**: explained by its appositive, *mutare.*
450. **penatibus**: cf. *Isthmo* (*v.* 299) and *tectis* (*v.* 380).　451. **at
quo**: Mss. have *ad quos.* Supply *me* as object of *remittis.* The question
is repeated in *v.* 459.　453. **quas peti terras iubes**: cf. Euripides,
Med. 502 ff. This sentence is quoted by Quintilian (I. O. 9, 2, 8) to
illustrate one use of the rhetorical question, which he says is used, ..."To
throw odium on the person addressed; as Medea says in Seneca, *Quas peti
terras iubes?*" This is one of the few bits of external evidence we have of
the authorship of the play.　456. **adulterum**: lover, i. e. Jason.
457. **Tempe**: a Greek acc. plural.　459. **exuli**: already an

nec das.   eatur.   regius iussit gener: 460
nihil recuso.   dira supplicia ingere:
merui.   cruentis paelicem poenis premat
regalis ira, vinculis oneret manus
clausamque saxo noctis aeternae obruat:
minora meritis patiar—ingratum caput,   465
revolvat animus igneos tauri halitus
hostisque subiti tela, cum iussu meo   469
terrigena miles mutua caede occidit;   470
adice expetita spolia Phrixei arietis
somnoque iussum lumina ignoto dare
insomne monstrum, traditum fratrem neci
et scelere in uno non semel factum scelus,
ausasque natas fraude deceptas mea   475
secare membra non revicturi senis:
per spes tuorum liberum et certum larem,   478
per victa monstra, per manus, pro te quibus
numquam peperci, perque praeteritos metus,   480

---

exile. **imperas nec das**: 'bricks without straw.'   462. **paelicem**:
a favorite word in the speech of Seneca's heroines. Here and in *v.* 495
Medea applies it with pathetic irony to herself, but usually it is a term of
reproach to a rival, as in *v.* 920.   469. **hostis subiti**: the *terrigenae*.
warriors who sprang into life full armed when Jason had sown the
dragon's teeth (cf. *v.* 169 n.; O. M. 7, 13¹). 470. **miles**: collective
(cf. *milite*, V. A. 2, 20). **occidit**: fell, perished.   471. **spolia Phrixei
arietis**: the golden fleece (*aurea pellis, v.* 361). It was Phrixus who
was carried on the ram's back to Colchis (see Cl. Dict., artt. *Phrixus*,
Helle).   473. **monstrum**: the sleepless dragon which guarded the
fleece in Colchis. It was drugged by Medea (O. M. 7, 149-156), who thus
enabled her lover to possess the prize. **fratrem**: Absyrtus.   Seneca
follows the more common version of his story; that being still a boy he
was carried away by Medea in her flight, and, when their father was about
to overtake them, was cut in pieces and his limbs thrown into the sea one
by one in order to delay the pursuit (cf. *vv.* 131 ff., 278, 963).
474. 'Crime done not once (but more than once) in one act of crime'—
i. e., not merely was the brother slain, but his body was mutilated and
to crown all cast unburied into the sea.   475. **natas**: sc.
Pelia (or *Peliae*). See *v.* 133 n.   479. **monstra**: the fire-breath-
ing bulls, the *terrigenae* (*v.* 470), the guardian serpent (*v.* 473).

per caelum et undas, coniugi testes mei,
miserere, redde supplici felix vicem. 482
aliena quaerens regna deserui mea: 477
ex opibus illis, quas procul raptas Scythae 483
usque a perustis Indiae populis agunt,
quas quia referta vix domus gaza capit, 485
ornamus auro nemora, nil exul tuli
nisi fratris artus: hos quoque impendi tibi;
tibi patria cessit, tibi pater, frater, pudor—
hac dote nupsi. redde fugienti sua.
IAS. Perimere cum te vellet infestus Creo, 490
lacrimis meis evictus exilium dedit.
MED. Poenam putabam: munus ut video est fuga.
IAS. Dum licet abire, profuge teque hinc eripe:
gravis ira regum est semper. MED. Hoc suades
mihi,
praestas Creusae: paelicem invisam amoves. 495
IAS. Medea amores obicit? MED. Et caedem
et dolos.
IAS. Obicere tandem quod potes crimen mihi?
MED. Quodcumque feci. IAS. Restat hoc unum
insuper,
tuis ut etiam sceleribus fiam nocens.

---

481. **coniugi**: gen. of *coniugium*. 482. **miserere**: used absolutely
—'Have pity.' **felix**: kindly. **redde.. vicem**: reciprocate. 483.
Scythae: Here and in *v.* 528 Medea calls her people by this name.
Being on the borders of Scythia the Colchians may be spoken of carelessly
as belonging to that race. . 485. **quas**: *et eas*—'And, as the palace,
filled with treasure, could hardly contain *these* riches (*opibus*), we adorned
the woods with gold.' The allusion is to the golden fleece, which was
hung upon a tree. 488. The first two feet may be treated as anapest-
anapest or as proceleusmatic-iambus (see Introd. p. 15, and cf 670 n.).
489. **redde .sua**: cf. *sunt hic sua praemia laudi*, V. A. 1, 461. For
the idea cf. Medea's demands of Creon in *vv.* 197, 272, 273. 490. The
truth of this pitiful plea of Jason's is confirmed by Creon's statement (*v.*
184). 492. **poenam putabam**: sc. *fugam*. Note the antithesis between
poenam and *munus*, and the strong irony of the latter. Cf. Ovid's expression, *Poenam pro munere poscis* (Met. 2, 99). 496. **obicit**: throw up

MED.   Tua illa, tua sunt illa: cui prodest scelus 500
is fecit—omnes coniugem infamem arguant,
solus tuere, solus insontem voca:
tibi innocens sit quisquis est pro te nocens.
IAS.   Ingrata vita est cuius acceptae pudet.
MED.   Retinenda non est cuius acceptae pudet. 505
IAS.   Quin potius ira concitum pectus doma,
placare natis.   MED.   Abdico eiuro abnuo —
meis Creusa liberis fratres dabit?
IAS.   Regina natis exulum, afflictis potens.
MED.   Non veniat umquam tam malus miseris
               dies   510
qui prole foeda misceat prolem inclitam,
Phoebi nepotes Sisyphi nepotibus.
IAS.   Quid, misera, meque teque in exitium
               trahis?
abscede quaeso.   MED.   Supplicem audivit Creo.
IAS.   Quid facere possim, loquere.   MED.   Pro
       me? vel scelus.   515
IAS.   Hinc rex et illinc— MED.   Est et his major
               metus:
Medea.   nos † confligere certemus sine,
sit pretium Iason.   IAS.   Cedo defessus malis.

---

as a reproachful reminder.   500. tua...fecit: cf. vv. 275, 276, 278.
501. arguant: cf. placeat, v. 288 n.   503. 'You should hold him guilt-
less who is guilty for your sake.'   504. cuius acceptae: cf. the
familar ab urbe condita of Livy, and translate, 'which one is ashamed of
having (so) received.'   507. placare: imperative. abdico, etc.: 'I
reject, forswear, disown them.'   510. non: With the optative subjunctive we should expect ne (cf. non Teucros agat, V. A. 12, 78).   512.
Phoebi: cf v. 28 n.   Sisyphi: The royal house of Corinth was de-
scended from Sisyphus, whose ancestry ran back through Aeolus, Hellen,
Deucalion and Prometheus to Iapetus, one of the original Titans. Com-
pared with the divine progeny of Phoebus his offspring would be foeda
(v. 511).   517. nos...sine: The reading here is corrupt and the sense
obscure. Perhaps the most satisfactory solution is found in making
certemus subordinate to sine and confligere to certemus: 'Let me (us)
strive to contend (with the king); let the prize be Jason.' Leo places a

et ipsa casus saepe iam expertos time.
MED.   Fortuna semper omnis infra me stetit. 520
IAS.   Acastus instat. MED. Propior est hostis
            Creo:
utrumque profuge.   non ut in socerum manus
armes nec ut te caede cognata inquines
Medea cogit: innocens mecum fuge.
IAS.   Et quis resistet, gemina si bella ingru-
            ant,   525
Creo atque Acastus arma si iungant sua?
MED.   His adice Colchos, adice et Aeeten ducem,
Scythas Pelasgis iunge: demersos dabo.
IAS.   Alta extimesco sceptra. MED. Ne cupias
            vide.
IAS.   Suspecta ne sint, longa colloquia am-
            puta.   530
MED.   Nunc summe toto Iuppiter caelo tona.
intende dextram, vindices flammas para
omnemque ruptis nubibus mundum quate.
nec deligenti tela librentur manu
vel me vel istum: quisquis e nobis cadet   535
nocens peribit, non potest in nos tuum
errare fulmen. IAS. Sana meditari incipe
et placida fare. si quod ex soceri domo
potest fugam levare solamen, pete.
MED. Contemnere animus regias, ut scis, opes 540
potest soletque; liberos tantum fugae
habere comites liceat in quorum sinu
lacrimas profundam.   te novi nati manent.
IAS.   Parere precibus cupere me fateor tuis:
pietas vetat; namque istud ut possim pati,   545

period after *configere*. 523. **caede cognata**: Acastus and Jason were
cousins.   529. **ne cupias vide**: 'Take care that ambition be not
your true motive.'   534. **deligenti...istum**: that discriminates between us.   545. **pietas**: cf. *v.* 438 n. **memet**: *Cogat* here has two

non ipse memet cogat et rex et socer.
haec causa vitae est, hoc perusti pectoris
curis levamen. spiritu citius queam
carere, membris, luce. MED. Sic natos amat?
bene est, tenetur, vulneri patuit locus.—   550
suprema certe liceat abeuntem loqui
mandata, liceat ultimum amplexum dare:
gratum est et illud. voce iam extrema peto,
ne, si qua noster dubius effudit dolor,
maneant in animo verba: melioris tibi   555
memoria nostri sedeat; haec ira data
oblitterentur. IAS. Omnia ex animo expuli
precorque et ipse, fervidam ut mentem regas
placideque tractes: miserias lenit quies. [*Exit.*]
MED. Discessit. itane est? vadis oblitus mei 560
et tot meorum facinorum? excidimus tibi?
numquam excidemus. hoc age, omnes advoca
vires et artes. fructus est scelerum tibi
nullum scelus putare. vix fraudi est locus:
timemur. hac aggredere, qua nemo potest   565
quicquam timere. perge nunc, aude, incipe
quidquid potest Medea, quidquid non potest.

　　Tu, fida nutrix, socia maeroris mei
variique casus, misera consilia adiuva.

objects, *memet* representing the person and the *ut* clause the act required.
It is a rare construction, two accusatives, or acc. of person and infinitive
representing the act, being more common.   547. **perusti**: seared In
v. 484 *perustis* had its more literal sense of sunburned, swarthy.   550.
tenetur: 'I have him.' **Sic...locus**: aside. For the thought implied
cf. *v.* 26 n.; see also Euripides, Med. 813.   551. **abeuntem**: agrees here
with the subject (*me*) of the infinitive. Instead of this the following constructions might have been used after *liceat:* (1) *abeunti loqui* (most
common), (2) *ut abiens loquar*, (3) *abiens loquar*, or (4) simply the infinitive, as in *v.* 542.   555. **melioris nostri**: my better self.   556.
haec: sc. *verba*.   560. **itane est**: For the spirit of the speaker see
v. 117.   562. **age**: addressing herself.   565. **hac...timere**: Attack at a point where none can conceive of danger—alluding again (cf. *v.*

est palla nobis, munus aetherium, domus 570
decusque regni, pignus Aeetae datum
a Sole generis, est et auro textili
monile fulgens quodque gemmarum nitor
distinguit aurum, quo solent cingi comae.
haec nostra nati dona nubenti ferant, 575
sed ante diris inlita ac tincta artibus.
vocetur Hecate.   sacra letifica appara:
statuantur arae, flamma iam tectis sonet.

CHORVS

Nulla vis flammae tumidive venti
tanta, nec teli metuenda torti, 580
quanta cum coniunx viduata taedis
    ardet et odit;

non ubi hibernos nebulosus imbres
Auster advexit properatque torrens
Hister et iunctos vetat esse pontes 585
    ac vagus errat;

non ubi impellit Rhodanus profundum,
aut ubi in rivos nivibus solutis
sole iam forti medioque vere
    tabuit Haemus. 590

caecus est ignis stimulatus ira
nec regi curat patiturve frenos
aut timet mortem: cupit ire in ipsos
    obvius enses.

26 n.) to the inhuman purpose gradually maturing in her mind.   571.
pignus...generis: an earnest of his descent (cf. the *pignora* demanded
by Phaethon, O. M. 2, 8).   575. **nati**: sc. *mei (nostri)*. **nubenti**: the
bride, who was said by the Romans to *veil* herself for her husband.
578. **arae**: in preparation for her invocation of the powers of darkness
(*v.* 740 ff.).   590. **Haemus**: a mountain range on the north of Thrace,
believed by the ancients to be of amazing height (cf. Pliny, N. H. 4, 18).
The thawing in spring of the deep snows which had fallen through the
winter would produce for rustic on-lookers in the distance very much the

parcite, o divi, veniam precamur,   595
vivat ut tutus mare qui subegit.
sed furit vinci dominus profundi
    regna secunda.

ausus aeternos agitare currus
immemor metae iuvenis paternae   600
quos polo sparsit furiosus ignes
    ipse recepit.

constitit nulli via nota magno:
vade qua tutum populo priori,
rumpe nec sacro violente sancta   605
    foedera mundi.

Quisquis audacis tetigit carinae
nobiles remos nemorisque sacri
Pelion densa spoliavit umbra,
quisquis intravit scopulos vagantes   610
et tot emensus pelagi labores
barbara funem religavit ora

same effect as if the range itself were melting away (*tabuit*).   596. **mare qui subegit**: Jason.   597. **vinci**: the subject is *regna*. **dominus profundi**: Neptune (cf. *profundi...dominator maris*, v. 4).   598. **regna secunda**: the sea (cf. *secundo maria sceptro regis*, Herc.Fur. 599; *secundum fluctibus regnum moves*, Phaedra 904). On the dethronement of Kronos (Saturn) by his sons the latter cast lots for the several portions of his dominions (Homer, Il. 15, 184 ff). Jupiter thus received the heavens, Neptune the *second* choice, the sea, and Pluto the third (cf. *tertiae sortis*, Herc. Fur. 609, 833), the unseen land of the dead.   599. **currus**: of the sun-god (O. M. 2, 107-110).   600. **iuvenis**: Phaethon (see O. M. 2, 1-328).   603. **constitit...magno**: has proved costly. *Magno* is abl. price.   604. **populo priori**: former generations.   605. **sacro...sancta**: *sacrosancta*, divided by *tmesis*. The sense is *inviolable, immutable*. **violente**: voc., best translated by an English adverb.   606. **foedera**: laws of nature. For the sentiment cf. *neve...naturae pollue foedus*, O. M. 10, 353. The particular law referred to here is that by which the gods were supposed to have confined man's sphere of conquest to the land and forbidden him the sea (cf. v. 385 n.; Horace, C. 1, 3, 21 ff.). In vv. 607-667 is given an account of the fate that befell several argonautic heroes.   610. **scopulos vagantes**: the Symplegades (cf. v. 342 n.; v. 456).   612. **barbara...ora**: Colchis.

raptor externi rediturus auri,
exitu diro temerata ponti
    iura piavit.   615

exigit poenas mare provocatum:
Tiphys in primis, domitor profundi,
liquit indocto regimen magistro:
litore externo, procul a paternis
occidens regnis tumuloque vili   620
tectus ignotas iacet inter umbras.
Aulis amissi memor inde regis
portibus lentis retinet carinas
    stare querentes.

ille vocali genitus Camena,   625
cuius ad chordas modulante plectro
restitit torrens, siluere venti,
cum suo cantu volucris relicto
adfuit tota comitante silva,
Thracios sparsus iacuit per agros,   630

613. externi...auri: the golden fleece.   **614. exitu:** abl. means, with *piavit*—by a dreadful end.   **617. in primis:** may be taken literally—among the first (in time)—or as the phrase *imprimis*, 'especially.' Tiphys lost his life before the Argo reached Colchis and was succeeded at the helm by Erginus (*indocto magistro, v.* 619), or, according to some accounts, by Ancaeus, a son of Neptune.   **622. Aulis...retinet carinas:** This possibly suggests the idea that the expedition against Troy had assembled at Aulis while Medea and Jason were still at Corinth. Tiphys (cf. *v.* 3 n., 617 n.) was a Boeotian, and the Boeotian port of Aulis (here personified) is represented as detaining the Greek fleet (or all ships) from running into the same perils which had cost him his life.   **624. stare querentes:** lamenting that they are not allowed to sail.   **625 ille:** Orpheus, who is said to have been the son of Apollo and the muse (*camena*) Calliope. The instances given here of his power to charm inanimate objects with his lyre are familiar. Ovid (M. 10, 1-77) tells of his passion for Eurydice and his descent into Hades to rescue her from death. It is said further that the women of Thrace, incensed at the bard's devotion to the memory of his lost wife, and consequent neglect of themselves, tore him in pieces (hence *sparsus...per agros*). The head (*v.* 631) floated down the Hebrus river and across the sea to Lesbos (O. M. 11, 1-60), thus transferring the power of lyric song to that island, where Alcaeus and

at caput tristi fluitavit Hebro:
contigit notam Styga Tartarumque,
    non rediturus.

stravit Alcides Aquilone natos,
patre Neptuno genitum necavit   635
sumere innumeras solitum figuras;
ipse post terrae pelagique pacem,
post feri Ditis patefacta regna,
vivus ardenti recubans in Oeta
praebuit saevis sua membra flammis,   640
tabe consumptus gemini cruoris
    munere nuptae.

stravit Ancaeum violentus ictu
saetiger; fratrem, Meleagre, matris
impius mactas morerisque dextra   645
matris iratae. meruere cuncti
morte quod crimen tener expiavit
Herculi magno puer inrepertus,
raptus, heu, tutas puer inter undas.

Sappho, the first lyric poets, afterwards lived and sang.   631. **tristi**: saddened by the burden it bore.   632. **notam**: because he had crossed it before, in quest of Eurydice (cf. O. M. 11, 61—*quae loca viderat ante*).   634. **Alcides**: Hercules. **Aquilone natos**: Calais and Zetes, the Boreades, called in *v.* 231 *sati Borea*. They were among the numerous victims of Hercules' prowess.   635. **Neptuno genitum**: Periclymenus (O. M. 12, 556-572).   637. **pacem**: conquest—peace by subjugation.   640. Cf. *vv.* 777, 778. The tragedy Hercules Oetaeus deals with this theme.   641. **gemini cruoris**: the blood of the centaur Nessus, mingled with the hydra's poison from Hercules' arrow.   642. **nuptae**: Deianira (O. M. 9, 141-272).   644. **saetiger**: the Calydonian boar.   645. **impius**: 'unnatural,' in slaying a relative. **moreris**: from *morior*. **dextra matris**: see Cl. Dict., artt. *Althaea, Meleager* (cf. *vv.* 779, 780; O. M. 8, 445-525). 646. **meruere...expiavit**: a confusion of two thoughts. It might be expressed either (1) *meruere cuncti poenam (mortem) qua crimen expiavit*, or (2) *commisere cuncti morte quod crimen expiavit*. In either case the thought is that having ventured upon the forbidden element all deserved the fate that had befallen Hylas, i. e. drowning.   648. **puer**: Hylas (see Cl. Dict.).   649. **tutas**: Not the stormy ocean but the quiet wa-

ite nunc, fortes, perarate pontum 650
    fonte timendo.

Idmonem, quamvis bene fata nosset,
condidit serpens Libycis harenis;
omnibus verax, sibi falsus uni
concidit Mopsus caruitque Thebis 655
ille si vere cecinit futura.
igne fallaci nociturus Argis 658
Nauplius praeceps cadet in profundum;
   *   * patrioque pendet 660a
      crimine poenas 660b

fulmine et ponto moriens Oileus;
coniugis fatum redimens Pheraei
uxor, impendens animam marito.
ipse qui praedam spoliumque iussit
aureum prima revehi carina, 665
ustus accenso Pelias aeno

---

ters of a spring, where none would look for danger. **651. fonte timendo:** abl. abs. of cause—'Since it is the spring that is to be feared, go, plow the ocean fearlessly' (*fortes*). **656 ille:** Mopsus, the seer. **659. Nauplius:** There are three of this name in the old mythology. Seneca here identifies the Argonaut with another of the name, the father of Palamedes, who was incensed at the treatment his son had received from the Greeks (V. A. 2, 82 ff.), and in revenge lured their returning fleet upon the rocks by means of a false beacon (*igne fallaci*). He is said to have met a like fate later, himself. See also the account given by the courier Eurybates in Agam. 558-570, where the expression *perfida face* is used. **660.** To preserve the Sapphic measure a half-line must be supplied, and Leo suggests *occidet proles*. **661.** It was Ajax, here called by his father's name Oileus, who perished *fulmine et ponto* on his way homeward from Troy (cf. V. A. 1, 43 ff.; Homer, Od. 4, 449 ff.). Our author here intimates that the real reason for his destruction was his father's offense in having sailed in the Argo (*patrio pendet crimine poenas*). **662. coniugis Pheraei:** Admetus, king of Pherae, whose wife Alcestis voluntarily gave up her life to save his (*impendens animam marito*), and thus helped atone for the sin of her father, Pelias, who had instigated the expedition of the Argo (*vv.* 664-665). This reading makes *uxor* a second subject of *pendet*. **664. ipse...Pe-**

arsit angustas vagus inter undas.
iam satis, divi, mare vindicastis:
parcite iusso.

lias: see *v.* 133 n.   667. **angustas...undas**: not the mighty waves of ocean but the bubblings of a caldron—a most unheroic fate (cf. *v.* 651 n.).   669. The chorus closes with an appeal to the angry gods to be satisfied with the fate of those who had fallen already and spare their leader Jason, who had merely obeyed orders. **iusso**: cf. Tro. 870: *ad auctorem redit sceleris coacti culpa.*

NVTR. Pavet animus, horret, magna pernicies
    adest.   670
immane quantum augescit et semet dolor
accendit ipse vimque praeteritam integrat.
vidi furentem saepe et aggressam deos,
caelum trahentem: maius his, maius parat
Medea monstrum. namque ut attonito gradu 675
evasit et penetrale funestum attigit,
totas opes effundit et quidquid diu
etiam ipsa timuit promit atque omnem explicat
turbam malorum, arcana secreta abdita,
et triste laeva † comprecans sacrum manu   680
pestes vocat quascumque ferventis creat
harena Libyae quasque perpetua nive
Taurus cohercet frigore Arctoo rigens,
et omne monstrum. tracta magicis cantibus
squamifera latebris turba desertis adest.   685
hic saeva serpens corpus immensum trahit
trifidamque linguam exertat et quaerit quibus
mortifera veniat: carmine audito stupet

670. The first two feet may be tribrach-anapest, or proceleusmatic-iambus (see Introd. p. 15, and cf. 488 n.). 671. **immane qauntum augescit**: 'how fearfully grows.' 673. **furentem**: sc. *Medeam;* so with *aggressam* and *trahentem.* 674. **caelum trahentem**: cf. *te quoque Luna traho,* O. M. 7, 207. 675. **attonito**: bewildered. 676. **penetrale funestum**: the unholy shrine (cf. *arae v.* 578). 677. **totas opes effundit**: is lavishing all her powers. All the principal verbs in the sentence (*effundit, promit, explicat, vocat*) are present tense. The nurse is looking on and describing what she sees. 678. **etiam ipsa**: There were powers which even Medea had shrunk from invoking before, but now fears and scruples alike are forgotten. 680. **laeva**: with the left hand, as ill-omened. 682, 683. **Libyae, Taurus**: extremes of climate. Medea's power ranged over them all. 687. **exertat**: *exsertat.*

tumidumque nodis corpus aggestis plicat
cogitque in orbes. 'parva sunt' inquit 'mala   690
et vile telum est, ima quod tellus creat:
caelo petam venena. iam iam tempus est
aliquid movere fraude vulgari altius.
huc ille vasti more torrentis iacens
descendat anguis cuius immensos duae,   695
maior minorque, sentiunt nodos ferae
(maior Pelasgis apta, Sidoniis minor)
pressasque tandem solvat Ophiuchus manus
virusque fundat; adsit ad cantus meos
lacessere ausus gemina Python numina.   700
et Hydra et omnis redeat Herculea manu
succisa serpens, caede se reparans sua.
tu quoque relictis pervigil Colchis ades,
sopite primum cantibus, serpens, meis.'

   Postquam evocavit omne serpentum genus, 705
congerit in unum frugis infaustae mala:
quaecumque generat invius saxis Eryx,
quae fert opertis hieme perpetua iugis
sparsus cruore Caucasus Promethei.

---

quaerit: sc. *eos.*   **693. fraude vulgari**: such arts as the common
herd can use.   **695. anguis**: the constellation Draco.   **696. ferae**:
the *arctoe.*   **697.** The constellation *ursa major* was known to the
Greeks in Homer's time (Il. 18, 487; Od. 5, 275), while *ursa minor*, though
long known to the Phoenicians, was not pointed out to the Greeks till the
time of Thales.   **698. solvat Ophiuchus**: 'let the serpent-holder
(Bootes) relax his close grip '—i. e., release the serpent.   **699. virus**:
acc.   **700. ausus**:, which dared. **gemina numina**: Apollo and Diana.
The former was the slayer of the python, and the oracle at Delphi, where
the encounter took place, was sacred to him alone, though here his sister
is associated with him in the exploit. Cf. the extension of the epithet
tonantibus to Juno in *v.* 59.   **702. caede...sua**: Whenever one of the
hydra's heads was lopped off, two grew up in its place.   **703. tu...
serpens**: the sleepless dragon (cf. *insomne monstrum, v.* 473 n.) which
guarded the golden fleece in Colchis.   **706. frugis**: To the venom of
serpents she now adds the juices of poisonous plants.   **707. Eryx**:

et quis sagittas divites Arabes linunt 711
pharetraque pugnax Medus aut Parthi leves 710
aut quos sub axe frigido sucos legunt 712
lucis Suebae nobiles Hercyniis:
quodcumque tellus vere nidifico creat
aut rigida cum iam bruma discussit decus 715
nemorum et nivali cuncta constrinxit gelu,
quodcumque gramen flore mortifero viret,
quicumque tortis sucus in radicibus
causas nocendi gignit, attrectat manu.
Haemonius illas contulit pestes Athos, 720
has Pindus ingens, illa Pangaei iugis
teneram cruenta falce deposuit comam;
has aluit altum gurgitem Tigris premens,
Danuvius illas, has per arentes plagas
tepidis Hydaspes gemmifer currens aquis, 725
nomenque terris qui dedit Baetis suis
Hesperia pulsans maria languenti vado.
haec passa ferrum est, dum parat Phoebus diem,
illius alta nocte succisus frutex;
at huius ungue secta cantato seges. 730
    Mortifera carpit gramina ac serpentium
saniem exprimit miscetque et obscenas aves
maestique cor bubonis et raucae strigis

the well-known mountain in Sicily.　711. **divites:** an epithet frequently applied to the Arabs (cf. H. C. 3, 24, 2: Epist. 1, 6, 6, etc.). **linunt:** smear, here poison.　713. **Suebae:** fem., as if those who dealt in witchcraft and poisons would naturally be women.　725. **gemmifer:** Claudian, writing in the fourth century of our era, spoke of the *gemmis Hydaspeis* (*de III Consulatu Honorii*, 4).　726. **nomen... dedit:** The *provincia Baetica*, in which was Corduba, Seneca's native city, received its name from the stream.　727. **Hesperia:** a general term for western—in the direction of *Hesperus*, the evening star. To the Greeks it sometimes meant Italian (cf. V. A. 1, 530). Here, as often to the Romans, it meant Spanish (cf. H. C. 1, 36, 4).　728, 729. Some herbs must be gathered at dawn, others at night.　731 ff. Cf. the witches' song over the caldron in *Macbeth* 3, 4, 1-38.　731. **serpentium:** the regular form of the gen. plur. In *v.* 705 *serpentum* is written for

exsecta vivae viscera. haec scelerum artifex
discreta ponit; his rapax vis ignium,   735
his gelida pigri frigoris glacies inest.
addit venenis verba non illis minus
metuenda. sonuit ecce vesano gradu
canitque. mundus vocibus primis tremit.

[*Medea calls upon all the powers of evil, and especially Hecate, to aid in her vengeance upon her rival.*]

MED.   Comprecor vulgus silentum vosque ferales
            deos   740
et Chaos caecum atque opacam Ditis umbrosi
            domum,
Tartari ripis † ligatos squalidae Mortis specus.
supplicis, animae, remissis currite ad thalamos
            novos:
rota resistat membra torquens, tangat Ixion humum,
Tantalus securus undas hauriat Pirenidas.   745
gravior uni poena sedeat coniugis socero mei:
lubricus per saxa retro Sisyphum volvat lapis.
vos quoque, urnis quas foratis inritus ludit labor,
Danaides, coite: vestras hic dies quaerit manus.
nunc meis vocata sacris, noctium sidus, veni   750

metrical reasons (cf. V. A. 12, 848).   **734. scelerum artifex**: Medea
(cf. *v.* 121 n.).   **735. discreta ponit**: separates, distinguishes.
737. verba: magic incantations.   **739. mundus tremit**: nature
shudders. 742. Cf. *alligat*, V. A. 6, 439.   **743. supplicis**: for
suppliciis, abl. abs. with *remissis*. The lines following give details.
thalamos novos: of Jason and Creusa (for a possible sense of *novos* cf.
v. 894 n.).   **745. Pirenidas**: acc. plural of *Pirenis*, adjective from
Pirene, the name of a famous fountain at Corinth. Tantalus is variously
described as having been king of Lydia, of Phrygia, of Argos and of Corinth. Our author evidently adopts the last version here.   **746. socero**:
Creon, who, as another king of Corinth, is named in connection with Tantalus.   **749. vestras...manus**: The Danaides had slain their hus-
bands, and the crime which Medea contemplated was worthy of them.
750. vocata...veni: The participle agrees with *tu*, the subject of *veni*,
and is feminine because Hecate, not *sidus*, is the thought-antecedent of
tu; *induta* and *minax*, *v.* 751, have the same agreement. **sidus**: apposi-

pessimos induta vultus, fronte non una minax.

    Tibi more gentis vinculo solvens comam
    secreta nudo nemora lustravi pede
et evocavi nubibus siccis aquas
egique ad imum maria, et Oceanus graves 755
interius undas aestibus victis dedit;
pariterque mundus lege confusa aetheris
et solem et astra vidit et vetitum mare
tetigistis, ursae. temporum flexi vices:
aestiva tellus floruit cantu meo,   760
coacta messem vidit hibernam Ceres;
violenta Phasis vertit in fontem vada
et Hister, in tot ora divisus, truces
compressit undas omnibus ripis piger.

    Sonuere fluctus, tumuit insanum mare 765
tacente vento; nemoris antiqui domus
amisit umbras, vocis imperio meae
die reducto; Phoebus in medio stetit
Hyadesque nostris cantibus motae labant:
adesse sacris tempus est, Phoebe, tuis.   770

Tibi haec cruenta serta texuntur manu,
    novena quae serpens ligat,
tibi haec Typhoeus membra quae discors tulit,

---

tive to *tu.* **751. fronte non una:** cf. *triformis, v.* 7 n. **752.** Having finished the solemn invocation Medea recounts the wonders she has wrought with the aid of these powers. **more gentis:** with *solvens.* **753. nudo...pede:** cf. *nuda pedem,* O. M. 7, 183. **758. et solem et astra:** i. e., at the same time. **vetitum tetigistis:** cf. *v.* 404 n. **759. temporum.. vices:** the seasons. I have caused spring flowers to bloom in summer, grain to ripen in winter, and water to flow up hill. **763. Hister:** the Danube in its lower course. **tot ora:** cf. Tacitus, Ger. 1, 3; Pliny, N. H. 4, 24. **768. in medio:** in mid-heaven. **769. Hyades:** taken as a representative constellation. **labant:** falter in their course. **771. tibi:** for thee, i. e., for Hecate. **cruenta:** abl. **772. novena...ligat:** each bound with nine serpent-coils *Novena* agrees with *serpens; quae* is acc. plur. **773. discors:** rebellious.

qui regna concussit Iovis.
    vectoris istic perfidi sanguis inest,   775
        quem Nessus expirans dedit.
Oetaeus isto cinere defecit rogus,
        qui virus Herculeum bibit.
piae sororis, impiae matris, facem
        ultricis Althaeae vides.   780
reliquit istas invio plumas specu
        Harpyia, dum Zeten fugit.
his adice pinnas sauciae Stymphalidos
        Lernaea passae spicula.
sonuistis, arae, tripodas agnosco meos   785
        favente commotos dea.

      Video Triviae currus agiles,
    non quos pleno lucida vultu
    pernox agitat, sed quos facie
    lurida maesta, cum Thessalicis   790
    vexata minis caelum freno
    propiore legit. sic face tristem
    pallida lucem funde per auras,

Typhoeus: one of the *gigantes* (cf. *v.* 410 n.).   **775. vectoris**: Nessus the centaur, who served as ferryman at the river Evenus (cf. *v.* 641 n.). **777**. Cf. Herc. Oet. 725 ff.   **779. impiae**: cf. note on *impius, v.* 645. **facem**: the fire-brand on whose preservation Meleager's life depended (cf. *v.* 645 n.). With *ultricis Althaeae* cf. *matris iratae, v.* 646. It is fitting for Medea, about to slay her children, to think of Althaea, who had caused the death of her son.   **782. dum...fugit**: cf. O. M. 7, 2-4; V. A. 3, 211-213.   **785. tripodas**: (*a* short) acc. plur. of the Greek *tripus*. **787-842**. Here follows a rhapsody in anapests, which fairly entitles the speaker to the epithet *maenas* used by herself in *v.* 806 and applied to her by the chorus in *v.* 849.   **787. Triviae**: Hecate, so called because her shrines were frequently placed at points where *three* roads met.   **790. lurida**: nom. **maesta**: abl. **Thessalicis minis**: An eclipse of sun or moon was a cause of great terror in ancient times, and when one occurred attempts were made to avert the catastrophe it was supposed to threaten by the beating of drums and the blowing of trumpets (cf. Tacitus, Ann. 1, 28, 3; Juvenal, Sat. 6, 442).   **791. caelum...legit**: sweeps through the sky (cf. *pontum legit*: V. A. 2, 207).   **793. pallida**: nom.

horrore novo terre populos
inque auxilium, Dictynna, tuum   795
pretiosa sonent aera Corinthi.
tibi sanguineo caespite sacrum
sollemne damus, tibi de medio
rapta sepulchro fax nocturnos
sustulit ignes, tibi mota caput   800
flexa voces cervice dedi,
tibi funereo de more iacens
passos cingit vitta capillos,
tibi iactatur tristis Stygia
ramus ab unda, tibi nudato   805
pectore maenas sacro feriam
bracchia cultro.   manet noster
sanguis ad aras: assuesce, manus,
stringere ferrum carosque pati
posse cruores—sacrum laticem   810
percussa dedi.
quodsi nimium saepe vocari
quereris votis, ignosce precor;
causa vocandi, Persei, tuos
saepius arcus una atque eadem est   815
semper, Iason.
tu nunc vestes tinge Creusae,
quas cum primum sumpserit, imas

---

796. **pretiosa...aera**: 'Corinthian bronzes' were proverbially fine and
valuable. Here the word seems to mean musical instruments of bronze.
797. **caespite**: altar of turf.   806. **maenas**: appositive to the
subject of *feriam* (see *v.* 383 n.; *v.* 787 n.; *v.* 849). **sacro**: with *cultro*.
807. **manet**: from *manare*, not *manere*.   809. **caros...cruores**: another intimation of her purpose (cf. *vv.* 26 n., 550, 848). She calls upon
the sword to taste her own blood (cf *feriam bracchia, v.* 806), that it may
not hesitate when called upon to drink the same from the veins of her
sons.   810. **sacrum laticem**: her blood—fulfilment of the promise in
feriam, v. 806.   813. **ignosce**: sc. *mihi*, or take absolutely.   814.
Persei: voc. Hecate is so called as being the daughter of Perses and
granddaughter of Persa and Sol (cf. Statius, Theb. 4, 482; also *Perseides*

urat serpens flamma medullas.
ignis fulvo clusus in auro   820
latet obscurus, quem mihi caeli
qui furta luit viscere feto
dedit et docuit condere vires
arte, Prometheus.   dedit et tenui
sulphure tectos Mulciber ignes,   825
et vivacis fulgura flammae
de cognato Phaethonte tuli.
habeo mediae dona Chimaerae,
habeo flammas usto tauri
gutture raptas, quas permixto   830
felle Medusae tacitum iussi
servare malum.
adde venenis stimulos, Hecate,
donisque meis semina flammae
condita serva.   fallant visus   835
tactusque ferant, meet in pectus
venasque calor, stillent artus
ossaque fument vincatque suas
flagrante coma nova nupta faces.

    Vota tenentur; ter latratus .   840
audax Hecate dedit et sacros
edidit ignes face lucifera.

---

herbae, O. R. A. 263).   **820. auro:** of her gift to the bride.   **820-830.**
The poison she is concocting is described in its effect as if it were liquid
fire, and then the mythical sources of fire are enumerated.   **822. furta:**
the stealing of fire from heaven for man.   **viscere feto:** cf. Vergil's
fibris renatis, A. 6, 595-600.   **823. condere:** store up—here in the
golden ornament (cf. *condita, v.* 835).   **827. cognato:** Phaethon was
son and Medea granddaughter of the sun-god.   **831. tacitum:** latent.
835 ff. visus, tactus: acc. **artus:** nom.   **840. latratus:** Hecate
was represented sometimes as having three heads (cf. *triformis, v.* 7, and
especially *triceps*, O. M. 7, 194), one of a horse, one of a lion, one of a dog;
and more often as merely attended by dogs, whose barking announced her

Peracta vis est omnis: huc natos voca,
pretiosa per quos dona nubenti feras.
ite, ite, nati, matris infaustae genus,   845
placate vobis munere et multa prece
dominam ac novercam.   vadite et celeres domum
referte gressus, ultimo amplexu ut fruar.

CHORVS

Quonam cruenta maenas
praeceps amore saevo   850
rapitur?   quod impotenti
facinus parat furore?
vultus citatus ira
riget et caput feroci
quatiens superba motu   855
regi minatur ultro.
quis credat exulem?

flagrant genae rubentes,
pallor fugat ruborem,
nullum vagante forma   860
servat diu colorem.
huc fert pedes et illuc,
ut tigris orba natis
cursu furente lustrat
Gangeticum nemus.   865

approach (cf. Oed. 569: *latravit Hecates turba*; V. A. 6, 257).   843 ff.
The frenzy is gone, and there remains only sullen determination.   846.
placate: win.   848. **ultimo**: To her hearers the word would have
its ordinary sense, to herself another, far deeper.   849. **cruenta**:
nom. The sense may be literally 'blood-stained' (cf. *vv.* 806-810), or it
may refer to her past crimes—the murder of brother and uncle.   850.
amore saevo: her passion for Jason (cf *v.* 398 n.).   **854. riget**: is
set.   856. Does not stand on the defensive, but dares attack.   857.
Sc. *eam esse.*   858-865. The chorus observes Medea's intense emotion,

frenare nescit iras
Medea, non amores;
nunc ira amorque causam
iunxere: quid sequetur?
quando efferet Pelasgis   870
nefanda Colchis arvis
gressum metuque solvet
regnum simulque reges?
nunc, Phoebe, mitte currus
nullo morante loro,   875
nox condat alma lucem,
mergat diem timendum
dux noctis Hesperus.

---

evinced by change of color and uncertain gait (cf. *vv.* 882-389).   866,
867. Cf. Medea's own expression, *vv.* 397, 398.   871. **Colchis**: nom.,
referring to Medea.   874. 'Drive swiftly the sun-chariot.' Medea's
reprieve was to end with the day, hence the prayer that night might come
quickly.   876. **alma**: The epithet commonly applied to *dies, sol, lux*
and words of kindred sense here is given to *nox* (cf. Tro. 438).   878.
dux noctis: cf. *gemini praevia temporis, v.* 71.

ACT V

[*A messenger enters from the palace, with news of the catastrophe within.*]

NVNT. Periere cuncta, concidit regni status.
nata atque genitor cinere permixto iacent.   880
CHOR. Qua fraude capti? NVNT. Qua solent
    reges capi:
donis. CHOR. In illis esse quis potuit dolus?
NVNT. Et ipse miror vixque iam facto malo
potuisse fieri credo. quis cladis modus?
avidus per omnem regiae partem furit   885
ut iussus ignis: iam domus tota occidit,
urbi timetur. CHOR. Vnda flammas opprimat.
NVNT. Et hoc in ista clade mirandum accidit:
alit unda flammas, quoque prohibetur magis,
magis ardet ignis: ipsa praesidia occupat.   890
    NVTR. Effer citatum sede Pelopea gradum,
Medea, praeceps quaslibet terras pete.
    MED. Egone ut recedam? si profugissem
        prius,
ad hoc redirem. nuptias specto novas.

884. **quis cladis modus**: Mss. assign this question to the chorus. *Modus* may mean either manner or measure, probably the latter here (cf. *omnem, tota, urbi timetur*). 890. **praesidia**: The water. The fire is so fierce as to devour what ordinarily is a safeguard against it. 891. **Pelopea**: Pelops was the son of Tantalus (cf. *v.* 745 n.), and became king of Pisa in Elis. From his name the whole southern peninsula of Greece came to be called Pelops' island, *Peloponnesus.* Here the adjective is applied to Corinth either as the home of his father (*v.* 745 n.) or in the sense merely of Grecian (cf. V. A. 2, 193). 893. **egone ut recedam**: An indignant question, implying that the act is inconceivable (cf. *v.* 929). 894. **nuptias novas**: cf. *thalamos novos, v.* 748; *thalamis novis,* Tro. 900. A new kind of marriage in that the scene is to be one of mourning

quid, anime, cessas? sequere felicem impetum. 895
pars ultionis ista, qua gaudes, quota est?
amas adhuc, furiose, si satis est tibi
caelebs Iason.　quaere poenarum genus
haut usitatum iamque sic temet para:
fas omne cedat, abeat expulsus pudor;　　　　　900
vindicta levis est quam ferunt purae manus.
incumbe in iras teque languentem excita
penitusque veteres pectore ex imo impetus
violentus hauri.　quidquid admissum est adhuc,
pietas vocetur.　hoc age et faxis sciant　　　　905
quam levia fuerint quamque vulgaris notae
quae commodavi scelera.　prolusit dolor
per ista noster: quid manus poterant rudes
audere magnum?　quid puellaris furor?
Medea nunc sum; crevit ingenium malis.　　　　910
　　　Iuvat, iuvat rapuisse fraternum caput;
artus iuvat secuisse et arcano patrem
spoliasse sacro, iuvat in exitium senis
armasse natas.　quaere materiam, dolor:
ad omne facinus non rudem dextram afferes.　915
　　　Quo te igitur, ira, mittis, aut quae perfido
intendis hosti tela?　nescio quid ferox
decrevit animus intus et nondum sibi

instead of rejoicing.　897. You love him still if you are satisfied
with merely depriving him of his bride. **furiose**: masculine, agreeing
with *anime*.　898. **caelebs**: unwedded, single, widowed. Both *caelebs*
and *viduus* are used indifferently of widowed persons and those who never
have married.　899. **haut**: *haud*.　902. **languentem**: 'If you waver
in your purpose.'　905. **pietas vocetur**: in comparison with what is
contemplated now. **faxis**: *feceris*.　907. **prolusit**: took exercise by
way of preparation for greater deeds (cf. *proludens fatis*. Tro. 182).　910.
Medea nunc sum: cf. *v*. 171.　912. **arcano sacro**: the golden
fleece (cf. *arcanus aries*, Thy. 226).　913. **senis**: Pelias (*v*. 133 n˙).
915. **non rudem**: cf. *rudes, v*. 908. Her hand is no longer unpracticed
in crime.　916. **perfido hosti**: Jason, as in *v*. 920.　918. **nondum**:
Yet it is clear that the idea had occurred to her at least as far back as her

audet fateri.   stulta properavi nimis:
ex paelice utinam liberos hostis meus   920
aliquos haberet—quidquid ex illo tuum est,
Creusa peperit.   placuit hoc poenae genus,
meritoque placuit: ultimum, agnosco, scelus
animo parandum est—liberi quondam mei,
vos pro paternis sceleribus poenas date.   .   925
  Cor pepulit horror, membra torpescunt gelu
pectusque tremuit.   ira discessit loco
materque tota coniuge expulsa redit.
egone ut meorum liberum ac prolis meae
fundam cruorem?   melius, a, demens furor!   930
incognitum istud facinus ac dirum nefas
a me quoque absit; quod scelus miseri luent?
scelus est Iason genitor et maius scelus
Medea mater—occidant, non sunt mei.—
pereant? mei sunt.   crimine et culpa carent,   935
sunt innocentes: fateor, et frater fuit.
quid, anime, titubas?   ora quid lacrimae rigant
variamque nunc huc ira, nunc illuc amor
diducit?   anceps aestus incertam rapit;
ut saeva rapidi bella cum venti gerunt   .   940
utrimque fluctus maria discordes agunt
dubiumque fervet pelagus, haut aliter meum
cor fluctuatur.   ira pietatem fugat
iramque pietas—cede pietati, dolor.

interview with Jason (vv. 549, 550), and hints of her growing purpose
are given in vv. 565, 848.   920. **paelice**: Creusa (cf. 462 n.).   922.
Creusa peperit: She first wishes that her rival had left children behind her, and then exclaims that Jason's children (though her own as
well) must now be thought of as Creusa's.   923. **ultimum**: crowning.
926 ff. With this wavering between right and wrong impulses cf.
Ovid's account of Medea's reflections at first sight of Jason (M. 7, 9-99),
and Dido's hesitation in yielding to her passion for Aeneas (V. A. 4, 1-55).
928. The fury of the outraged wife gives way to the tender affection of
the mother. **tota**: probably nom. 931. **incognitum**: unheard-of.
936. **frater**: sc. *meus*. Absyrtus had been innocent and yet was sacri-

Huc, cara proles, unicum afflictae domus   945
solamen, huc vos ferte et infusos mihi
coniungite artus.   habeat incolumes pater,
dum et mater habeat—urguet exilium ac fuga.
iam iam meo rapientur avulsi e sinu,
flentes, gementes osculis—pereant patri,   950
periere matri.   rursus increscit dolor
et fervet odium, repetit invitam manum
antiqua Erinys—ira, qua ducis, sequor.
utinam superbae turba Tantalidos meo
exisset utero bisque septenos parens   955
natos tulissem!   sterilis in poenas fui—
fratri patrique quod sat est, peperi duos.

     Quonam ista tendit turba Furiarum impotens?
quem quaerit aut quo flammeos ictus parat,
aut cui cruentas agmen infernum faces   960 .
intentat?   ingens anguis excusso sonat
tortus flagello.   quem trabe infesta petit
Megaera?—cuius umbra dispersis venit
incerta membris?   frater est, poenas petit—
dabimus, sed omnes.   fige luminibus faces,   965
lania, perure, pectus en Furiis patet.

     Discedere a me, frater; ultrices deas
manesque ad imos ire securas iube:
mihi me relinque et utere hac, frater, manu

---

ficed, why not her sons as well?   950. **pereant**: be lost to.   954.
turba Tantalidos: the brood of Niobe, who was the mother of seven
sons and seven daughters (O. M. 6, 182).   956. **sterilis fui**: My two are
not enough. Another shade is given the thought in the following verse—
as if in slaying her sons she were sacrificing one each to her father and
her brother.   959. **quo ..parat**: 'Against whom are they preparing
to direct their fiery darts?'   961. **anguis**: cf. *v*. 14.   962. **trabe**:
torch (cf. *facem, v*. 15).   964. **incerta**: indistinct (cf. *incertam lunam*,
V. A. 6, 270).   965. **sed omnes**: My atonement shall be complete.
fige faces: Thrust fire-brands into my eyes, tear, burn. The sudden
apparition of her murdered brother throws her into a frenzy of rage and
despair.   967. **ultrices deas**: the Furies (cf *v*. 18 n.; also *ultrices Dirae*,

quae strinxit ensem—victima manes tuos   970
placamus ista.   quid repens affert sonus?
parantur arma meque in exitium petunt.
excelsa nostrae tecta conscendam domus
caede incohata.   perge tu mecum comes.
tuum quoque ipsa corpus hinc mecum aveham. 975
nunc hoc age, anime: non in occulto tibi est
perdenda virtus; approba populo manum.   [*Exit.*]

[*Enter Jason, hurrying with those who answer his
call to attack the house of Medea.*]

JAS.   Quicumque regum cladibus fidus doles,
concurre, ut ipsam sceleris auctorem horridi
capiamus.   huc, huc fortis armiferi cohors   980
conferte tela, vertite ex imo domum.
MED.   [*Appearing upon the housetop.*]   Iam iam re-
          cepi sceptra germanum patrem,
spoliumque Colchi pecudis auratae tenent:
rediere regna, rapta virginitas redit.
o placida tandem numina, o festum diem,   985
o nuptialem!   vade, perfectum est scelus;
vindicta nondum: perage, dum faciunt manus.
quid nunc moraris, anime?   quid dubitas potens?
iam cecidit ira.   paenitet facti, pudet.

V. A. 4, 473).   970. **victima...ista**: One of her sons, who is slain at this
point.   974. **tu**: to the living child.   978. Jason appears on the
scene, calling upon the loyal subjects of Creon to avenge the death of their
king and their princess. He does not see Medea till *v.* 995, and
is recognized by her first in *v.* 992. **regum**: Creon and his daughter.
quicumque: subject of *doles*.   980. **armiferi**: voc. **cohors**:
appositive to *armiferi*.   982-984. 'I have recovered all I gave up for
my lover'—i. e,, this moment of vengeance is worth them all. She had
reminded Jason in their interview of what she had lost for his sake, enu-
merating essentially the items given here (cf. *vv.* 477-489).   984.
redit: contracted from *rediit* (cf. *peti, v.* 248).   985. **placida**: pro-
pitious.   987. **perage**: sc. *vindictam.*   988. **quid dubitas potens**: 'Why do you hesitate, having the power?'   989. A momentary

quid, misera, feci? misera? paeniteat licet,   990
feci—voluptas magna me invitam subit,
et ecce crescit. derat hoc unum mihi,
spectator iste. nil adhuc facti reor:
quidquid sine isto fecimus sceleris perit.
IAS.   En ipsa tecti parte praecipiti imminet.   995
huc rapiat ignes aliquis, ut flammis cadat
suis perusta. MED.   Congere extremum tuis
natis, Iason, funus, ac tumulum strue:
coniunx socerque iusta iam functis habent,
a me sepulti; natus hic fatum tulit,   1000
hic te vidente dabitur exitio pari.
IAS.   Per numen omne perque communes fugas
torosque, quos non nostra violavit fides,
iam parce nato. si quod est crimen, meum est:
me dedo morti; noxium macta caput.   1005
MED.   Hac qua recusas, qua doles, ferrum exigam.
i nunc, superbe, virginum thalamos pete,
relinque matres. IAS.   Vnus est poenae satis.
MED.   Si posset una caede satiari haec manus,
nullam petisset. ut duos perimam, tamen   1010
nimium est dolori numerus angustus meo.

feeling of regret, giving way almost immediately (*v*. 991) to a fierce joy at
sight of her husband and thought of his grief. **991. invitam**: in spite
of myself. **992. derat**: *deerat* (cf. *derit*, *v*. 403). **hoc**: explained by
its appositive *spectator iste*, i. e., Jason, whom she now sees approaching.
993. nil...reor: As he had not seen the death of his first son it counted
for nothing (see next verse, and cf. *vv*. 275-280, 500, 501). **994.
perit**: probably perfect (cf. *redit*, *v*. 984)—is lost, is wasted. **995.
ipsa**: nom.—Medea. **998. funus**: for *rogum*. **999. iusta...func-
tis**: the service due the dead (cf. *iusta Troiae*, Tro. 65). *Functis* is for
defunctis. In sending her fiery gift to Creusa, and by that means destroy-
ing the royal palace with all it contained, Medea had provided for the
cremation of Jason's wife and father-in-law, and she now tauntingly chal-
lenges him to carry out his threat (*v*. 996) to burn her house, and so per-
form the same rites for his sons 1000, 1001. **hic, hic**: pointing to
the dead and to the living boy. **1006. hac**: here in the body of our
son. **ferrum exigam**: cf. *ferrum exigatur*, *v*. 125 n.   **1009. una**

IAS. Iam perage coeptum facinus, haut ultra
    precor, 1014
moramque saltem supplicis dona meis. 1015
MED. Perfruere lento scelere, ne propera, dolor:
meus dies est: tempore accepto utimur.
IAS. Infesta, memet perime. MED. Misereri
    iubes.
bene est, peractum est. plura non habui, dolor,
quae tibi litarem. lumina huc tumida alleva, 1020
ingrate Iason. coniugem agnoscis tuam?
sic fugere soleo. patuit in caelum via:
squamosa gemini colla serpentes iugo
summissa praebent. recipe iam natos, parens;
ego inter auras aliti curru vehar. [*Flies away.*] 1025
IAS. Per alta vade spatia sublimi aethere,
testare nullos esse, qua veheris, deos.

caede: *unius caede.* 1015. supplicis: *suppliciis.* dona: imperative. 1017. meus dies est: i. e., the day granted her by Creon (*v.*
295); so *tempore accepto.* At this point she strikes the second of her sons,
and thus provokes Jason's despairing cry, *memet perime* (*v.* 1018).
1022. sic: in a chariot drawn by dragons (see next verse, and cf. O. M.
7, 220). 1024. 'Parent take back your children now.' With this
parting taunt she throws the bodies down to Jason, and herself mounts
her aerial chariot.

The Journal Co.,
Printers.
Crawfordsville, Ind.

CPSIA information can be obtained at www.ICGtesting.com
Printed in the USA
LVOW070423230712

290999LV00001B/35/P

9 781141 663163